The Wise Owl Guide to…
Dantes Subject Standardized Test

Introduction to World Religions

Printed in the United States of America

ISBN-10: 1441406522
ISBN-13: 9781441406521
Library of Congress Control Number: 2009925791

Cover design © Heath Anderson

INTRODUCTION 8
ABOUT THE TEST 8
PART I. DEFINITION AND ORIGINS OF RELIGION 9
BASIC DIMENSIONS OF RELIGION 9
APPROACHES TO RELIGION 9
PART II. INDIGENOUS RELIGIONS 11
NATIVE SOUTH AMERICAN TRADITIONS 11
THE MAYANS 11
NATIVE MIDDLE EASTERN TRADITIONS 15
SACRIFICES AND MAGIC 15
DIVINATION AND ASTROLOGY 15
THE SUMERO-AKKADIAN PANTHEON 16
THE BABYLONIAN MYTHS AND EPICS 16
HELLENIC / GREEK TRADITIONS 19
TEXTS 19
THE GODS AND THEIR MAIN FUNCTIONS 19
HOMERIC PANTHEON 20
MORE POWERFUL THAN THE GODS 21
GREEK/ROMAN BELIEFS 21
ROMAN TRADITIONS 22
THE GODS AND THEIR MAIN FUNCTIONS 22
ETRUSCAN INFLUENCED CHANGES 23
ROME AND GREECE 23
GREEK AND ROMAN MYTHOLOGY TODAY 23
ABORIGINAL RELIGION 24
THE RAINBOW SERPENT 24
NATIVE NORTH AMERICAN RELIGION 25
THE SHAMAN 25
CEREMONIES 25
AFRICAN RELIGION (VOODOO) 26
SHINTOISM 27
MIXED SHINTO 27
THE SHINTO WARRIOR 27
PART III. HINDUISM 29
HISTORICAL DEVELOPMENT 29
RIG-VEDA 29
SAMA-VEDA 30
YAJUR-VEDA 30
ATHARVA-VEDA 30
VARNA (CLASS SYSTEM) 31

UPANISHAD PHILOSOPHY 31
REINCARNATION AND KARMA 32
DOCTRINE AND PRACTICE 33
THE THREE DEBTS 33
TEN COMMITMENTS 33
THE FOUR GOALS IN LIFE 34
THE THREE PATHS TO MOKSHA (SALVATION) 35
THE YUGAS 37
THE SIX ACCEPTABLE PHILOSOPHIES 38
IMPORTANT FIGURES OF LATER HINDUISM 40
HINDUISM IN PRACTICE 42
PRACTICES 43
LATER HINDUISM RELIGIOUS MOVEMENTS 43
MAJOR HINDU HOLIDAYS 45
SOCIAL REFORM FOR LATER HINDUISM 45
PART IV. BUDDHISM 47
HISTORICAL DEVELOPMENT 47
THE FOUR PASSING SIGHTS 47
RENOUNCING THE HOME AND A SIX-YEAR QUEST ... 48
ENLIGHTENMENT 48
ASSEMBLING THE RELIGION AND THE CONVERTS 48
BUDDHA'S PARINIRVANA AND BUDDHISM SPREAD .. 49
MAJOR TRADITIONS 51
MAJOR IDEAS 51
KARMA 52
THE THREE REFUGES 52
THE FOUR NOBLE TRUTHS 52
DOCTRINE AND PRACTICE 55
MAHAYANA BUDDHISM 55
PURE LAND 56
MEDITATIVE SCHOOLS (CHAN AND ZEN) 56
RATIONAL SCHOOLS (TIAN-TAI) 56
ESOTERIC/MYSTERY SCHOOLS (ZHEN-YAN AND
SHINGON) 56
PART V. CONFUCIANISM 57
HISTORICAL DEVELOPMENT 57
DOCTRINE AND PRACTICE 58
FILIAL PIETY: XIAU (HSIAO) 58
SOCIAL PHILOSOPHY 58
POLITICAL PHILOSOPHY 59
CONFUCIANISM AND EDUCATION 59

TEACHERS AND CRITICS OF CONFUCIANISM 59
CONFUCIANISM TODAY 60
PART VI. TAOISM 61
HISTORICAL DEVELOPMENT 61
DOCTRINE AND PRACTICE 61
THE PHILOSOPHY OF THE *DAO DE JING* 61
DAOISM/TAOISM IN PRACTICE 63
THE EIGHT IMMORTALS 63
PART VII. JUDAISM 65
HISTORICAL DEVELOPMENT 65
ABRAHAM 65
MOSES 66
EARLY RITUALS 67
SPREADING TERRITORY 68
THE HEBREW PROPHETS 68
JERUSALEM 69
EXILE 69
THE JEWS AND HELLENISTIC INFLUENCE 70
JERUSALEM'S FALL 70
BAR KOCHBA 70
DENOMINATIONS 71
HISTORIC JEWISH GROUPS 71
CURRENT JEWISH DENOMINATIONS 72
FIXING THE CANON 73
TALMUD 74
HOLOCAUST (SHOAH) 74
DOCTRINE AND PRACTICE 74
MAJOR HOLIDAYS 74
PRACTICES 78
PART VIII. CHRISTIANITY 82
HISTORICAL DEVELOPMENT 82
THE TWELVE APOSTLES 83
JESUS' TEACHINGS 83
THE LAST SUPPER 84
THE CRUCIFIXION AND RESURRECTION 84
JUDAIZERS AND HELLENISTS 85
EMPEROR CONSTANTINE 85
RELIGIOUS FREEDOM 85
INQUISITIONS 85
MAJOR TRADITIONS 87
MAJOR BRANCHES 87

DOCTRINE AND PRACTICE 91
  THE NEW TESTAMENT 91
  MAJOR HOLIDAYS 92
  PRACTICES 94
  TRINITY 95
PART IX. ISLAM 96
  HISTORICAL DEVELOPMENT 96
    MUHAMMAD'S SUCCESS 96
    CALIPHS (632-661) 96
  MAJOR TRADITIONS 98
  DOCTRINE AND PRACTICE 99
    PRACTICES 99
    MAJOR BELIEFS 101
    DENOMINATIONS (SECTS) 103
  GLOSSARY 108
LIST OF APPENDICES: 139
  APPENDIX A: MAJOR GREEK AND ROMAN GODS 140
  APPENDIX B: MAJOR HINDU GODS 141
  APPENDIX C: INDIAN CASTE SYSTEM (HINDU) 142
  APPENDIX D: BUDDHISM: A QUICK LOOK 143
    FOUR NOBLE TRUTHS 143
    NOBLE EIGHTFOLD PATH 143
    THREE CHARACTERISTICS OF EXISTENCE 143
    BUDDHISM'S VALUES AND VIRTUES 144
    BUDDHISM'S BELIEFS ON WHAT BINDS US TO
    SAMSARA (REINCARNATION) AKA. THE TEN FETTERS
    (SAMYOJANA) 144
  APPENDIX E: BOOKS OF THE BIBLE 145
    OLD TESTAMENT (ALSO THE JEWISH TANAKH) 145
    NEW TESTAMENT 147
  APPENDIX F. CHRISTIAN SEVEN DEADLY SINS 149
  APPENDIX G. MAJOR CHRISTIAN DENOMINATIONS ... 150
  APPENDIX H: APPROXIMATE PERCENT OF
  EXAMINATION 152
BONUS TAKING THE RELIGION TEST! 154
  STEP 1. RIGHT NOW - TODAY! 154
  STEP 2. TOMORROW! 154
  STEP 3. THE DAY BEFORE THE TEST! 154
  STEP 4. THE NIGHT BEFORE THE TEST! 155
  STEP 5. THE DAY OF THE TEST 155
  STEP 6. FEELING A BIT TENSE? 155

TAKING THE TEST 157
   TEST TIP #1 - QUESTION TYPES................................ 157
   TEST TIP #2 - INTERPRETING PROBLEMS.................. 157
   TEST TIP #3 – TIME 158
   TEST TIP #4 - "QUESTIONS AND ANSWERS" 158
   TEST TIP #5 – FINISHING IN STYLE!......................... 159
PRACTICE TEST.. 160
INDEX.. 189

INTRODUCTION

Are you going to learn EVERYTHING about the World Religions in this study guide? Absolutely NOT! But… are you going to learn enough to pass the DSST test? YES! In this book we focus on what you need to know, that is it. With the DSST (Dantes Subject Standardized Test) series tests the test is on what is most COMMONLY taught in a college course. That leaves out a lot of content of what COULD be taught. Expect to see some answers that you don't know. But, the goal isn't to get 100% (you should take a traditional class and invest lots of time, money, and effort to do that). The goal here is simply to pass. It has been my experience that no one cares WHERE I took my classes, just that I HAVE them and have a degree (a couple of them in fact). Prepare for this test with this study guide and you will be well on your way to a degree in significantly less time than hitting the books in night school (this is not to say it is any easier to get a degree this way, just more flexible)! This book is written in an easy-to-read, understand, and remember format. World Religions is a fascinating topic, and no matter if you have a test to pass or not this information will make you feel like a more educated person for knowing it. Even if you THINK you know everything there is to know about religions this book will teach you a thing or two!

ABOUT THE TEST

World Religions Dantes Subject Standardized Test (DSST) test covers similar material that is taught in a three-credit college lower level (general education) course.
The exam (and this book) covers topics such as:
- Definition and origins of religion
- Indigenous Religions
- Hinduism
- Buddhism
- Confucianism
- Taoism
- Judaism
- Christianity
- Islam

This test book includes a 100-question practice test to ensure you have a solid handle on the course information.

PART I. DEFINITION AND ORIGINS OF RELIGION

This test is divided among many areas of religion. This portion of your test will account for approximately six percent of the questions. Part I will cover:

- The basic dimensions of religion
- Approaches to religion

BASIC DIMENSIONS OF RELIGION

There are basic dimensions that show up in most religions from indigenous to present day. **Religion** is a system of beliefs (doctrines, rituals, and practices) that are designed to connect people with the sacred.

- A sense of **awe** in the Lord.
  - o Fearing retribution and hoping for blessings.
- **Anxiety** in rituals
  - o Has the Lord seen the rituals favorably and often enough?
- **Rituals** and **rites of passage**
  - o Examples are parenthood and marriage
- **Myths** and rituals
  - o Following past rites and rituals because it is what has always been done without knowing the exact origin or reason for the ritual.
- **Prayer** both individual and in-group settings.
- **Divination** determining future events based on magical practices and reading the divine's "signs".
- **Recognition of a supreme being.**
- **Taboo** or hands-off activities (i.e. sins).
- **Purification rites**
- **Sacrifices and gifts**

APPROACHES TO RELIGION

There are many approaches to the study of religion.

- Origin of religion
  - o Origin of religion is the study of religion in pre-history (i.e. before the written word).

- History of religion
  - Unconcerned with the theological claims the religion makes (except for their historical significance).
  - Topics of interest in the history of religion are:
    - Religious figures
    - Events
    - Evolution of doctrine
- Sociology of religion
  - Concerned with the social structure within a religion.
    - Relationship between the individual and the religious community.
  - Emile Durkheim was the forefather of this field of study.
    - Wrote a book called *The Elementary Forms of Religious Life,* which theorizes that, religion cannot be separated from society. The religion is a social reflection of the conditions of the society.
- Psychology of religion
  - Concerned with the psychological principles at work in religion.
  - Forefather is William James.
- Anthropology of religion
  - Concerned with the basic needs that religion fulfills.
- Cultural anthropology of religion
  - Concerned with the cultural aspects of religion (rituals, beliefs, arts, and practices of faith).
- Literary approaches
  - Study of sacred texts for metaphor, thematic elements, and character development.
- Neurological approaches
  - Scientific study of the brain of religious practitioners.

PART II. INDIGENOUS RELIGIONS

This portion of your test will account for approximately six percent of the questions. Part II will cover:

- Native South American traditions
- Native Middle Eastern traditions
- Hellenic and Roman traditions
- Australian Aboriginals
- Shintoism
- Native North American traditions
- African religion of Voodoo

NATIVE SOUTH AMERICAN TRADITIONS

Founded in 250 AD the Mesoamerican Mayan civilization (Southern Mexico, Guatemala, Belize) had impressive architectural structures (the temples, ceremonial courts, and highways). The Mayans were devout toward crops and what brings them about (maize and soil are spoke about in reverence). The religion (heavily influenced by the culture and religion of the Olmecs) lasted until about 900 AD, and then faced a significant decline. The Spanish converted most of the remaining Mayans to Roman Catholicism.

THE MAYANS

A polytheistic religion known for their temples, the Mayans, believed the dome of the sky was seven-layers with six ascending steps in the east, and six ascending steps to the west (thirteen compartments). Four gods were in charge of the sky, referred to as the **Bacabs**. The Bacabs were divided by color and direction:
- Red Bacab, East
- White Bacab, North
- Black Bacab, West
- Yellow Bacab, South

According to the Mayan culture it took three tries to create the world.
- The creator gods said "earth" and land appeared

- They produced vegetation and animals (none of which could offer thanks for the world).
- They produced higher creatures (made of mud) that were unintelligent but could speak (they later dissolved into the water).
- The creations from wood
  - These beings were unintelligent and could not give thanks for the world.
  - The other animals turned against these woodland creatures, however some escaped (becoming ancestor to the monkey).
- The creations from maize
  - These beings were too good and too equal to the gods, so they dulled them with some mist.
  - The gods gave these beings (humans) wives and the humans worshipped their gods.

THE MAYAN DEITIES

Mayan deities (each having a benevolent and malevolent side) had four types:
- Celestial and remote
  - Itzamná
    - Creator and lord of the day and night
    - Also the sun god Kinich Ahau
    - Benevolent
    - Most important and supreme
- Fertility and domestic
  - Related to everyday life
  - First mother shed blood, causing maize (humans made from maize).
  - Chac
    - Rain-god and fertility deity.
  - Ah Mun
    - God of all crops
  - Ixchel
    - Patroness of human fertility
- Death and war
  - Realm beneath the earth
  - Ah Puch
    - God of death
  - Ixtab

- Goddess of suicide
- Mayans believed that suicides went directly to heaven.
- Calendric and ceremonial
    - Sponsored by the thirteen compartments of heaven and nine of the lower world.

RITES OF PASSAGE

The rites of passage in the Mayan culture were surrounded by ceremony:
- Birth
    - Children were carried to the priest and the name was determined by horoscope, the father's family name, the combined family name of both parents, and a nickname.
- Toddler
    - Boys had a white bead tied to their hair to symbolize purity.
    - Girls wore a red shell tied to their waistband to symbolize purity.
- Puberty
    - Ceremony removing the purity symbols.
    - Boys moved to an unmarried man house but continued working for their fathers.
    - Girls remained at home and were considered marriage eligible.
- Marriages
    - Usually involved a matchmaker.
    - Involved a bride price.
    - Groom must work for brides father for a period of six to seven years.
- Funerals
    - Dead wrapped in cloth with maize and some money in their mouth.
    - Buried in the ground to feed the maize.

SACRIFICES

There were some human sacrifices in the Mayan culture. Usually young girls were sacrificed because of their purity. One of the types of sacrifices was to bind and throw a person into a well for several hours to speak to the rain gods with little chance of survival.

Bloodletting was also a ritual (even for the aristocracy). Usually shoving spines through the penis, ear, or a thorn cord through the tongue to draw blood, and the blood was applied to paper to collect and offer to the gods.

TEXTS

The Spanish destroyed most of the religious texts of the Mayans, however three main codices have survived, named after the cities in which they were kept:
- Dresden
    - Has a precise table of Venus and the moon to predict solar eclipses.
- Madrid
- Paris Codices

Other important texts that have been recovered are:
- Books of Chilam Balam
    - Historical chronicles of myth, divination, and prophecy.
- Ritual of the Bacabs
    - Religious symbolism
    - Medical incantations
- Popol Vuh
    - Mythology and cosmology
    - Chronicles creations of man, action of gods, origin and history of Quiche people
    - Royal chronology down to 1550

BELIEFS

Mayan royalty was considered semi-divine (intermediaries between the gods and the people). When royalty died they were given elaborate funerals.

The Mayans believed:
- Afterlife

- Most everyone went to the underworld (including royalty).
- Only ones to go to heaven were those that were sacrificed or those that died in childbirth.
- Science and religion
  - Science and religion are synonymous
  - Astronomy
    - Calculated solar year
    - Ability to predict solar eclipses
  - Math
    - Positional notation of zero
- Time
  - Believed the world had been created five times (and destroyed four).
  - There were lucky and unlucky days (the priests had to determine between the two).
    - Advised when to plant, harvest, and wage war.
  - Prediction of the world ending on December 21, 2012.

NATIVE MIDDLE EASTERN TRADITIONS

Mesopotamia was a country nestled between two rivers in the Middle East wrought with war and ever-changing religion.

SACRIFICES AND MAGIC

Babylonians believed in:
- Incantations
- Rituals and prayers
- Star reading

The priests in Babylonia were more powerful than the worshippers. From the beginning priests were able to organize religion like a business including accurate records and construction of large buildings (**ziggurats** – man built mountains) where they conducted rituals, schooling, and practiced divination.

DIVINATION AND ASTROLOGY

An entire group of priests specialized in the interpretation of signs, omens, and dreams. The priests devoted significant time to reading the omens in sheep's liver where they thought the intentions were on the surface of the liver.

Astrology was another significant pastime in divination. Those that studied the stars kept accurate records of the movements in the sky that paved the way for astrology today. Many religions relied heavily on the stars while practicing divination.

THE SUMERO-AKKADIAN PANTHEON

With over two thousand deities nearly every aspect of nature was represented. There were six deities that became geographical "gods" over large parts of the region. The more important gods in this religion were:

- **An** (Anu) the sky-god and chief deity of Uruk.
- **Enlil** (Bel) the air-god and became god of the lands beneath.
- **Nanna** (Sin), Enlil's son, was a moon-god in the region of Ur.
- **Utu** (Shamash) was the sun god in Larsa (and later when Larsa was destroyed Utu became god of Sippar).
- **Enki** (Ea) the water-god did double-duty as the wisdom-god and lived in Eridu.
- **Ninhursag** (Aruru, Nintu, Ninmah) was the mother god prevailing over Kish.

The gods were civil to one another; while there may have been a large temple in the god's region of origin there were likely smaller temples and/or sanctuaries for the other gods.

ISHTAR

Ishtar was the closest god in Mesopotamia to have been universally worshipped. A female god, Ishtar was a virginal love goddess, queen of fertility, and a woman warrior.

MARDUK OF BABYLON

Marduk was Ishtar's greatest rival for universally worshipped god. Marduk became universally known because Hammurabi (the sixth king of Babylon) made Babylon the capital of the kingdom. When Babylon was escalated to importance so was Marduk who then merged with many gods absorbing their attributes.

THE BABYLONIAN MYTHS AND EPICS

Babylonian myths and epics are vast, however many bare remarkable resemblance to many religions in the West.

CREATION

There are two theories in Mesopotamia of how life and earth was made. The first theory was what the Sumerians believed.

- The Sumerians believed that the sea (Nammu) existed first, and from that, heaven (An) and earth (Ki) emerged separated by air (Enlil).
- Then in order to see better Enlil created the moon-god (Nanna) and the moon-god created the sun god (Utu).
- When the air moved across the Earth it mixed with water and life was created.
- Humans were made from Nammu, Ninmah (mother Earth), and Enki (water-god).

The second theory believed the world was created by fight over the tablets of destiny. The dragons of darkness and chaos, led by the bird-god Zu (Tiamat), and the gods of light and order (Ninurta) struggled over control of the tablets.

- **Apsu** (god of fresh water) and **Tiamat** (dragon of unbounded salt water) combined to make all of the gods.
- The new gods were so active and Apsu wanted peace so against the wishes of Tiamat vowed to destroy the other gods.
- Ea destroyed Apsu upon hearing the plan, and Tiamat vowed revenge.
- Tiamat created monsters to avenge Apsu's death and Ea and Anu fled.
- Marduk fought Tiamat and split her in two forming parts of the Earth with her.
- Markuk made humankind from the blood of Kigsu (Tiamat's second husband).

FLOOD

That's right, you didn't think that Noah was the first to suffer a flood in religion did you? The original flood story was Sumerian and based on the floods of the rivers surrounding them. The theory was the gods were trying to punish humans for their sins. The plot to wipe out humankind was revealed to one man (Utnapishtim) by the god Ea and he advised Utnapishtim to build an ark.

ISHTAR'S DESCENT TO THE LAND OF THE DEAD

To resemble the seasons a myth of Ishtar was conceived.

- Ishtar went down to the netherworld to fetch her dead lover.
- Ishtar is admitted into the heavens but as she passes through the seven gates one by one her clothing and jewels are removed.
- Namtar (pest-god) afflicts her with sixty diseases.
- The upper world begins to grow listless and dull, they cannot reproduce, and fertility has left the earth.
- Ea commands that Ishtar be brought back to life (Namtar sprinkles the water of life upon her).
- Ishtar is restored and health returns to the earth.

THE JOURNEY OF GILGAMESH

The story begins with Gilgamesh (ruler of the city of Uruk (Erech)) and his friendship with a wild man Enkidu.

- Enkidu dies young because he offended Ishtar.
- Gilgamesh searches for immortality and finds the herb that grants immortality (with the help of Utnapishtim).
- A serpent robs Giglamesh of the immortality herb.

For the Babylonians the moral of the story was that there as no hope of a great afterlife. It was best to enjoy the life you have.

Hellenic / Greek Traditions

The formation of Greek religion (spanning from Minoan to Mycenae periods to the days of its Roman Empire conquest) started with the northern invasions of the territory. With the grouping of so many different peoples and cultures the religion was formed through a combination of many. Different cities worshipped different deities through sacrifices.

The Indo-European invaders gave at least three gods:
- Zeus (sky-father and rainmaker)
  - For the Romans this was Jupiter.
- Demeter (earth-mother)
- Hestia (virgin goddess of the hearth, and sister of Zeus.
  - For the Romans this was Vesta.

The Hellenics contributed many gods including:
- Athena
- Hermes

The Greeks did not fear their gods and they weren't far removed. Sacrifices were made, and permissions asked for rituals and rites of passages, but it was more of a cooperative gesture.

Texts

The major texts attributed to the Greek literature that speaks of the gods are *The Iliad* and *The Odyssey* (both written by Homer). The poet Hesiod wrote *Theogony* with the goal to synthesize the Greek gods by introducing the Twelve Olympians and describing Night and Time's role in creation.

The Gods and Their Main Functions

Greece focused on separating people and isolating them according to beliefs. However, once the northerners invaded, a single language and intermingling of the religions developed. There were several gods that served different functions:
- Zeus
  - Rain maker and sky-god
  - In many areas he was the god of fertility
  - Some territories he also ruled the underworld

- o Fathered many heroes and kings
- o He had other wives, but Hera was the most permanent.
  - Hera
    - o Wife of Zeus
    - o Became the patroness of married women.
  - Apollo
    - o Before he became a sun-god he was associated with agriculture.
    - o Sponsored athletics
    - o He was an archer that would pierce men with blood and sickness.
    - o God of healing until his son Aesculapius took over.
    - o He displaced Delphi (and absorbed his abilities of revelation).
    - o Only later was he associated with the sun and the golden chariot.

HOMERIC PANTHEON

The Homeric epics helped to unify the regional religions and beliefs of Greece. The gods congregated to Mount Olympus (which was no longer considered a mountaintop, but somewhere in the heavens). At Mount Olympus, Zeus (born to Kronos and Rhea), reigned king and father of the god family. Some of the more prominent members of Zeus' family were:

- Zeus's most loved daughter, Athena (goddess of wisdom).
- Zeus's most loved son, Apollo (archer-god) with the power to heal and harm.
- Ares, the war loving son that Zeus scolds often.
- Artemis is the shy goddess of wild animals that often hides in the mountains.
- Aphrodite. Zeus' daughter with Dione, is the goddess of love (married to her half brother Hephaestus – a son of Zeus and Hera).
- Hermes, child of Zeus and Maia, was the messenger god who could be naughty.
- Poseidon is the god of the seas and full brother of Zeus.
- Hades (Pluto) is the god of the underworld and full brother of Zeus.

MORE POWERFUL THAN THE GODS

The Greeks believed that Moira (fate) was more powerful than the gods. Other powers more mighty than the gods were:

- Blind Folly
- Terror
- Strife
- Turmoil
- Rumor
- Death

GREEK/ROMAN BELIEFS

THE UNIVERSE

The Greeks believed the Earth was a flat disk floating in the ocean with its own body and soul. In Hesoid's Theogony four divine beings were first to exist:

- Chaos
- Abyss
- Earth (Gaea)
- Love (Eros)

The Earth was created when it was taken from her consort Heaven (Uranus) (by Uranus' son, Cronus, by cutting Uranus' genitals) so that she may give birth.

SPIRITS, MONSTERS AND OTHER MYTHOLOGICAL BEINGS

Gods weren't the only beings present in Greek/Roman mythology. Others of note are:

- **Amazons** (female warriors)
- **Keres** (evil female spirits)
- **Medusa** (female monster with hair made of snakes)
- **Satyrs** (half-man, half-goat nature spirits who followed Dionysus)
- **Centaurs** (half-man, half-horse creatures who were wild but knowledgeable)
- **Sirens** (half-bird, half-woman with an irresistible song that caused mariners to crash on the rocks of their island)

While death was not generally feared, it was not seen as a celebration. Very few are punished after death, and very few were thought to reach paradise after death.

- Hades
    - General destination of most of the dead.
    - Cold, damp, and dark place.
    - Gates guarded by Cerberus (fearsome dog).
    - Without proper burial one cannot enter the gates.
    - The river Styx is the boundary between earth and Hades.
- Tartarus
    - Deepest region of underworld.
    - Only the most evil wind up here.
    - It is also a place where the monsters go once defeated by the gods.
- Elysium (Elysian Fields, Elysian Plain)
    - Paradise only for the distinguished.

ROMAN TRADITIONS

The Roman religion came from humble beginnings. The religion of "Numa" was a religion closely resembling magic. People believed in charms, taboos, and omens that gods and some people possessed. Numen was found in inanimate objects, people, and was transferable. For the Romans the gods didn't have human-like characteristics (gender, heredity, and history). Therefore, art largely ignores them because there was nothing to sculpt, draw, or paint.

THE GODS AND THEIR MAIN FUNCTIONS

The major gods in Rome were Jupiter, Mars and Quirinus, and Janus and Vesta.

- Jupiter (Optimus Maximus)
    - God of lightning, thunder, and rain.
    - Predetermined fate for people and gave them birds to read as omens.
    - His lightening was typically used as punishment.
    - In Rome his temple was built on the Capitoline hill.
- Mars and Quirinus
    - Two war gods (in Greece this was Ares).

- Janus and Vesta
  - Janus was the keeper of the door, god of beginnings (January).
  - Vesta was invoked at the ending of ceremonies as he represents the god of endings.

ETRUSCAN INFLUENCED CHANGES

When Rome fell under Etruscan dominance in the sixth century B.C. there were changes in their religious customs and beliefs.

- Jupiter was linked to Juno as husband and wife (the first marriage among the Roman gods).
- Minerva was introduces and was parallel to Athena (goddess of wisdom, arts, and trades). Later she was called to aid during wartime and was represented wearing a helmet, and holding a spear and shield.

ROME AND GREECE

The priests began to consult the oracles (Cumean Sibyl) from the Sibylline Books stored in the Capitoline temple during the sixth century B.C.. The priests would consult the oracles and report to the people how to move forward without divulging what verses they reviewed. Many of the verses prescribed were unfamiliar to the Romans because they were Greek in origin. The Romans began to adopt many of the Greek rituals and beliefs. Some of the influences of these verses were:

- Erection of temples.
- Identifying Roman with Greek gods (i.e. Poseidon as Neptune, Hermes as Mercury, and Aphrodite as Venus).
- Humanizing the gods (giving them characteristics).

GREEK AND ROMAN MYTHOLOGY TODAY

As Christians began to assume power the Greek and Roman religions were eradicated, which began Europe's Dark Ages. The European Renaissance was the rediscovery of the Greek and Roman religion, philosophy, and culture. Today, many ancestors of the Greek and Roman religion are Orthodox Christians.

ABORIGINAL RELIGION

There are 400 distinct groups of Aborigines across Australia. Each has their individual myths. The characteristics of most of the Aborigine tribes are:

- Creation happened during Dreamtime.
    - o Dreamtime is when their ancient ancestors journeyed to the blank lands and as a result animal, plant, mountains, and rivers developed.
    - o The routes taken during Dreamtime by the Creator Beings are linked together by sacred sites that cross the country.
- The religion and culture is more of an oral library within the people.
- They believe that people should be land centered (not human centered). The idea that humans are temporary and land is not.
- Sites of land hold subtle feelings as an intangible reality.

THE RAINBOW SERPENT

A common myth in Aboriginal religion is the rainbow serpent. The rainbow serpent is said to live in Australia water, and descended from the Milky Way. This serpent is responsible for:

- Shaping landscapes
- Drowning people
- Rainmaking
- Healing
- Causing weakness, illness and death

NATIVE NORTH AMERICAN RELIGION

The Native North American Religion is largely oral (considered preliterate, or primal) that focuses on hunting and agriculture. The universe is divided into heaven, earth, and the underworld. While Native Americans may have believed in many spirits, none was considered mightier than the Great Spirit.

THE SHAMAN

A common practice in Indian religion, **shamans** are spiritual people that act as intermediaries between the spirit and physical world. Through drumming, fasting, or sometimes use of psychotropic substances shamans enter a trance to communicate with the spirit world.

However, in many Native American religions many men and some women went on **vision quests** (communicative rite of passage journeys with the spirit world). Therefore, at times the only difference between the shaman and the people were the number of spirit guides contacted by the shamans.

CEREMONIES

- Sweat Lodge ceremony
  - Thermal bath for spiritual cleansing.
- Vision Quest
  - Rite of passage contacting spirit world.
- Sun Dance Ceremony
  - Important festival contrived of dancing, singing, drumming, and sometimes piercing of chest and back.
- Smudging
  - Blowing or fanning smoke over a person to please the Great Spirit.
- Making of Relations
  - Almost a form of adoption ceremony, to ensure no one is alone and they become a part of a family.
- Sacred Pipe
  - Connecting physical and spirit world.
- Ghost Dance
  - Dance signifying regeneration of the Earth.

AFRICAN RELIGION (VOODOO)

Voodoo can be traced back to the West African Yoruba people, and as slavery was introduced in the west, so was Voodoo. Voodoo is nothing like Hollywood portrays it. A book by St. John called *Haiti or the Black Republic* is responsible for most of the myths of Voodoo today.

VOODOO BELIEFS

Each Voodoo group worships a different spiritual group of deities (**Loa**).

- The god of the gods is God Olorun, and he authorized the God Obatala to create earth and life.
- The lesser Yoruba deities were also called **orishas**.
- They had a quarrel and God Obatala was temporarily banished.
- There are hundreds of minor spirits.
  - o The earlier ones are called **Rada**.
  - o The ones that originated later (often named after leaders) are called **Petro**.

SIMILARITIES BETWEEN CATHOLICISM AND VOODOOISM

- Both religions focus on a Supreme Being.
- The Loa are similar to Christian saints because they are given a special attribute.
- Both religions believe in an afterlife.

VOODOO SOUL

The soul has two parts:
- **Gros bon ange** (big guardian angel)
- **Ti bon ange** (little guardian angel)
  - o Leaves the body during sleep or ritual.
  - o Can be damaged or captured by evil when not in body.

SHINTOISM

Shintoism is the native religion of Japan. Shintoists believed (as written in the book *Kojiki*) that the Japanese islands and its inhabitants were created by the gods (the primal male, **(Izanagi)** and primal female, **(Izanami)**). They traveled from heaven via a Floating Bridge and Izanagi pushed his spear into the mud, Izanami gave birth to the eight islands of Japan. Then Izanami bore 35 deities, the last one, (Kagu-Tsuchi) the heat god, killed Izanami during birth. Izanagi raged and hacked Kagu-Tsuchi into bits, and each bit became another god.

After some time Izanagi went to fetch Izanami back from the underworld (**Land of Yomi**), however he waited too long and she was covered in maggots. She (and several gods) chased him and he blocked the way from the underworld. After he escaped the Land of Yomi he cleansed himself. Upon cleansing his left eye he produced the highest Japanese deity, **Amaterasu**, the goddess of the sun.

MIXED SHINTO

As time progressed and Buddhism influenced Japan, Daoism, and yin-yang magic Shinto became something a little different. Shinto:
- Extended the family concept
  - Basic family clan system is at the heart of Japanese culture.
  - Family shrine (**uji-gami**) typically a long ago ancestor sought for protection and assistance .
  - **Dosojin** were road side pillars that took on fertility and protective themes (vulva and phallus).
- Hospitality to guests
  - Villages were welcoming of visiting deities (such as the Buddhist and Daoist deities).

THE SHINTO WARRIOR

The Shinto warrior (**samurai**) practiced the **Bushido** code. The Bushido code had eight attitudes:
- Loyalty
  - First loyalty to the Emperor.
  - Second to the lord the samurai serves.

- Gratitude
  - Living a right life is an expression of gratitude.
- Courage
  - Surrender life readily for the one you serve.
- Justice
  - Do not allow selfishness to stand in the way of duty.
- Truthfulness
  - Not even to spare someone hurt.
- Politeness
  - Even to the enemy.
- Reserve
  - Never show feeling despite how much is felt.
- Honor
  - Death is preferred to disgrace.
  - A knight carried two swords, one for the enemy and one to kill himself in the case of defeat.
  - **Harakiri (seppuku)** self-disembowelment carried out without emotion.
  - Women cut their jugular veins in an action called **jigai**.

Part III. Hinduism

This portion of your test will account for approximately ten percent of the questions. Part III will cover:

- Historical development
- Doctrine and practice

Historical Development

Hinduism was founded in 1500 B.C. or even earlier. The Aryans inhabited India and brought with them their customs and culture. The Aryans had separate tribes and each tribe had a leader (**rajah**). The rajah maintained a private army to protect his people and gathered priests to obtain blessings from the gods. The people of the region had roles and responsibilities:

- The father (**pitar**) was the head of the family.
- The wife and mother (**matar**) were free to do as she wished and ruled her home however she wished.
- Daughters were free from having to marry, and could marry whom they chose.

The Aryans took some time to settle because for the most part they were a wandering people. Aryans began to create epics and stories that shaped their religion. From these epics are Hinduism's earliest writings, the **samhitas** (four of them):

- Rig-Veda
- Sama-Veda
- Yajur-Veda
- Atharva-Veda

Rig-Veda

The oldest of the Veda, it is ten books that contain thousands of hymns. The hymns were to the deities found on earth, heaven, and air. The Aryans did not worship in structures; they worshipped outside in full view of the heavens. In the center of their worship they prepared as many as three fires.

The priests had specific jobs during the ceremonies. For example:

- **Hotar** called down to the gods to enjoy their sacrifices.

- **Adhvaryu** built the altar and prepared the sacrifice.

- **Agnidh** kindled the sacrificial fire.

- **Brahmin** the most important priest that represented the prayer.

There were many gods that were introduced in early Hinduism *Rig-Veda*:

- **Indra**

  - One of the most prevalent gods was Indra (ruler of the gods of the mid-region), god of storms, and rainstorms that end the dry season. Indra was the god of war as well.

- **Rudra (Shiva)**

  - Greatly feared god.

  - Also presided over the healing plants in the mountains.

- **Ushas**

  - Goddess of dawn.

- **Vishnu**

  - Not a major player in the Rig-Veda, but became a more prominent god in later Hindu culture.

- **Varuna**

  - He was the judger of truth, lies, and sin.

  - People prayed forgiveness from sin to Varuna.

SAMA-VEDA

Sama-Veda is a collection of chants for the priests for sacrifices (mostly borrowed from the hymns of the *Rig-Veda*).

YAJUR-VEDA

Yajur-Veda is a supplemental to supply prayers to be accompanied with the *Rig-Veda*.

ATHARVA-VEDA

The *Atharva-Veda* is an independent collection of charms and spells.

Varna (Class System)

The Aryan's invasion of the Ganges valley caused many different kinds of people to inhabit the same area. In these areas the non-Aryans were below the Aryans in the social order. There formed four distinct social groups:

- **Brahmins** were the priests.

- **Kshatriyas** (Rajanyas) were the rulers.

- **Vaisyas** were the common people.

- **Shudras** were the servants (non-Aryans).

Marriage and strong social ties between these classes was forbidden and the Brahmins and Kshatriyas were at conflict for the top class.

Upanishad Philosophy

Upanishad was the new philosophy that began to develop. Upanishad means "sitting near" and it represented sitting near a sage and listening to his teachings.

Inner reflection in lieu of ritual and sacrifice began to become more popular. The thinkers were beginning to outnumber the priests and become more powerful. The soul (**atman**) was viewed as having a higher worth than matter (**prakriti**). Therefore, the sacrifices were not as important as meditation.

Monism

Many Upanishad thinkers believed in **Monism** (the dualism between atman (soul) and prakriti (matter/natural world)). They found dualism between earth happenings with inner soul happenings. For example, the light that shines on earth is the same light that shines in our souls and heats our inner fire (which is why we feel warm when we are touched).

Brahman

For the Upanishad thinkers Brahman represents the Supreme Being. Brahman is formless and actionless a being of creative power and is the world of reason, feeling, will and self-consciousness.

Reincarnation and karma started with the Upanishad philosophy and shaped later Hinduism.

- **Samsara** (reincarnation)
  - o Birth-death-rebirth belief.
  - o Based on the belief that he soul (atman) never dies.
  - o With only one exception (if the soul becomes one with Brahman), the soul re-manifests in different beings.
  - o The rebirth can be in heaven, hell, any form of being, and any type of being.

- **Karma** (deeds)
  - o The future existence of the soul depends on how ethical the person lives their present life.
  - o Karma reinforced the caste system because people believed that if someone was born to a slave or a ruler it was due to karma.

DOCTRINE AND PRACTICE

There was a shift from the open sacrifices at the alters to the reflection of within (**tapas** – inner fire). In order to release the inner spirit came the development of yoga. However, many **Brahmins** (priests) did not adopt the practice of inner-reflection (their place in the caste system was at risk). The Brahmins adapted and began:

- Performing marriages
- Presiding over births and deaths
- Taught in homes (as **gurus**)
- Held household worship ceremonies (**pujas**)

The Hindu people of today are still very ritualistic in their homes. The Brahmins tradition of celebrations, rituals, and pilgrimages still live on in the Hindu culture.

The **Dharma Shastras** are the law codes of Hinduism. These instructions guide Hindus in all manners of life (religious and non). The main subjects are:

- Codes of conduct
- Civil and criminal law
- Punishment and atonement

THE THREE DEBTS

Hindus believe there are three debts in life:

- Debt to God.
- Debt to sages and saints.
- Debt to ancestors.

TEN COMMITMENTS

The doctrine if Hinduism is based off of ten commitments:

- Ahimsa (no harm)
- Satya (no lies)
- Asteya (no stealing)

- Brahmacharya (no overindulgence)

- Aparigraha (no greed)

- Saucha (cleanliness)

- Santosha (contentness)

- Tapas (self-discipline)

- Svadhyaya (study)

- Ishvara Pranidhana (surrender to the gods)

THE FOUR GOALS IN LIFE

The Brahmins believed the **Dharma** (sacred law) outlines all allowable human pursuits within their lives.

KAMA (PLEASURE)

- Specifically pleasure attained through love.

- **Kamasutra** is instruction in the art of love.

- **Natyasastras** is instruction in the literary arts.

- Desire and gratification is not seen as a forbidden.

ARTHA (SUBSTANCE)

- To attain material possessions (high social status and riches).

- It is known that to attain these things one must be ruthless and this goal is not frowned upon..

DHARMA

- Religious and moral law.

- Considered more fulfilling than kama and artha.

- Willing to sacrifice individual ideals and wealth for the betterment of society.

- Instruction is identified in the Code of Manu and the Dharmasastras.

- o Women in these instructions are seen as people that can help their wavering brothers, husbands, and fathers back to the path of righteousness.
- o Women are also seen as one of the greatest temptations to veer them off the path to dharma.

MOKSHA

- The release from the reincarnation cycle.
- Referred to as **nirvana.**

THE THREE PATHS TO MOKSHA (SALVATION)

Based on Hindu beliefs there are three methods to achieve salvation (**moksha**), they are recognized as the three paths (**margas**).

THE WAY OF WORKS (KARMA MARGA)

- Stresses rituals and age-old customs.
- Followed by most of the Hindus.
- Study the Vedas.
- Be hospitable to his fellow man.
- *Code of Manu*
  - o Book of instruction for Karma Margo.
  - o Stresses rites of passage.
  - o Observe caste system (do not marry outside the caste, observe social regulations, and do not break the dietary rules set out for the caste system).
  - o Honor the deities of the household and the woman of the house presents the first portion of the meal to the household deities.
- **Shraddha** rites - death rites
  - o **Pinda** (food-balls made up of rice) offered to the ancestral spirits to strengthen them.
- Women's role in the Way of Works
  - o Serve men meekly.

- o Household duties are a priority.
- o Worship her husband regardless of his personal traits.
- o Never marry again if her husband dies before her.

THE WAY OF KNOWLEDGE (JNANA MARGA)

- Only the major thinkers (Upanishads) followed this method.
- The belief that the cause of human misery is ignorance (**Avidya**).
- Philosophies that the Way of Knowledge typically uses are Sankhya, Yoga, and Vedanta (to be explained in the next section).
- The ideal life is in four stages (**ashramas**):
  - o Student of religion (**brahmacharga**)
    - ▪ Boy sent off to a teacher's home to study for an indefinite point of time.
    - ▪ Teacher doesn't supply him with food, the student must go from home to home begging for food.
    - ▪ Developing character and acquiring knowledge is the goal.
  - o Married man and householder (**grastha**)
    - ▪ Leave home of the teacher, go back to family, and marry.
    - ▪ No breaking of caste dietary rules.
    - ▪ Focus on family, career, and other worldly pursuits.
  - o **Vanaprastha**
    - ▪ When children reach adulthood.
    - ▪ Focus on religion and other spiritual things.
  - o **Sannygasu** (holy wanderer)

- Giving up all earthly ties (name, status, possessions).

- After the ritual the status cannot be reclaimed, it is seen as death.

- Only the top three castes can seek the initiation ceremony.

- The wife will become a widow by holy abandonment or the man may make her **sannyasini** and be celibate companions.

THE WAY OF DEVOTION (BHAKTI MARGA)

The ordinary people that practiced Hinduism largely follow the way of devotion (**bhakti**). The common people could not follow the way of knowledge and didn't have the capabilities to meditate on their souls for long, they respected those that could, but could not follow their ways to seek salvation.

- ***Bhagabad Gita*** (*Song of the Blessed Lord*) most influential literary work of bhakti..

  o Contains one hundred thousand couplets telling tales of Aryan clans.

  o Dictates that the other two ways are good, but bhakti is superior in seeking salvation.

The way of devotion is open to all genders and castes, which makes it an attractive choice for the ordinary people.

THE YUGAS

Hindus believe that there are four **Yugas** (ages) for the world that restart in a cyclic pattern. Each Yuga has specific characteristics and the cycle of our make up what is called a **divya-yuga**.

- **Satya Yuga** (krta-yuga)

  o Golden age

  o Meditation on Visnu.

  o Average lifespan is 100,000 years and most of the population is good.

  o Lasts 1,728,000 years.

- **Treta Yuga**
    - Silver age
    - Performance of **vajnas** (sacrifices).
    - Average lifespan is 10,000 years and the goodness decreases by a quarter.
    - Lasts 1,296,000 years.

- **Dvapara Yuga**
    - Bronze age
    - Worship of deities in temples.
    - Lifespan is 1,000 years and goodness decreases by half.
    - Lasts 864,000 years.

- **Kali Yuga**
    - Iron Age
    - Marked by hypocrisy and quarreling.
    - Chanting of Holy Names of the Lord.
    - Lifespan is 100 years and goodness reduced to twenty-five percent.
    - By the end the lifespan will be twenty and only food will be meat.

Kalpas is the theory of the destruction and recreation of the world. Based on this theory the world goes away at the end of every **kalpa** (large period of time). The souls depart and become suspended. After a time of rest (**pralaya**) the world is recreated. This cycle repeats over and over again.

The Six Acceptable Philosophies

There are six main systems of the view of nature (**darshana**). The three with the greatest reflect on religion are; Sankhya, Yoga, and Vedanta.

This system is the opposite of the monism practiced by the Upanishads. The Sankhya philosophy recognizes only two categories of being:

- Matter (**prakriti**), when organized becomes the natural world.

- Souls (**purusha**).

Neither category is considered illusion. The presence of purusha activates prakriti. The activity of the natural world comes in three modes:

- **Sattva**, associated with white, good and wise with insight.

- **Rajas**, associated with red, passion.

- **Tamas**, associated with darkness, moody.

Depending on someone's traits at the time is how much they are influenced by one of the three modes of activity. For example, if someone is passionate they are most influenced by rajas at the time.

Souls are viewed not as one that we return to, but each as independent and eternal. Souls are free and should be detached. However, the presence of souls attracts the prakriti elements (**tattvas**), and as souls gain insight (**buddhi**) they realize they need to detach to allow true freedom.

THE YOGA SYSTEM

Yoga combines physiological and psychological aspects to help the psyche contemplate. Yoga is largely special postures, breathing, and repetition to help the practician concentrate on their inner thoughts. The practice of Yoga has eight steps:

- Abstains from harming living things, deceit, theft, and unchastity.

- Cleanliness, calm, study, and prayer.

- Sitting the proper posture

- Breath regulation

- **Samadhi** (trance) where the mind is no longer thinking of anything and has become one with the Ultimate.

The Vedanta is the conclusion of the Veda. There are three versions of this system:

- Shankara's Non-Dualism – **Advaita**
  - o Prakriti and the ego, **Jiva**, aren't one or together, they are incomprehensible to the human.

- Ramanuja's Qualified non-dualism – **Vishisht-Advaita**
  - o The physical world, individual souls, and Supreme Being are real, non-divisible.
    - The physical world and souls is the way the Supreme Being manifests.
  - o The Supreme Being
    - His name is Vishnu, and is omnipotent, all-powerful, and merciful.
    - He reveals himself in five ways:
      - To the souls in heaven sitting on a serpent (**Shesha**).
      - Accumulation of knowledge.
      - Through the ten avataras.
      - Living in the human heart.
      - The images that people make of him.

- Madhva's Dualism – **Dvaita**
  - o Souls and gods are not one in the same.
  - o The souls that are saved go to heaven to be with Vishnu and the others spend eternity in hell.
  - o Salvation comes through Vayu the wind-god (son of Vishnu)
    - Vayu breathes his life into those he saves

IMPORTANT FIGURES OF LATER HINDUISM

There are several deities and beings that are significant for Hinduism. **Trimurti** is the belief in three great deities (Brahma, Vishnu, Shiva) together performing creation, preservation, and destruction. Common people found it hard to comprehend the worshipping of three gods, and typically chose to worship one god at a time.

- Brahma
    - The Creator, worshipped the least, but deeply respected.
    - Physical/human characteristics:
        - King with four heads
        - Reading the Vedas
        - Riding a white goose
        - Aloof
- Shiva
    - The Destroyer, in order to make room for new creation.
    - God of the mountain where healing herbs found.
    - Became known as the fertility god.
- Vishnu
    - The Preserver, always king, perfect, simple, and patient.
    - Physical characteristics
        - Four arms
        - In his hands he holds the mace, discus, conch, and lotus.
        - He wears a crown.
        - His feet are blue, his vest yellow.
    - His spouse is the goddess of fortune and beauty Lakshmi.
    - Vishnu returns to Earth in the form of Avatars (ten of them). Most popular Avatars:
        - Rama – the ideal man
        - Krishna – a war hero, and erotic

The numbers of the actual deities that are worshipped are significant (in the millions). The common people visit shrines according to their specific needs.

HOLY PLACES

Ordinary Hindus perform pilgrimages to holy places. Rivers are seen as particularly holy (the most holy is the Ganges river). There are two types of holy places:

- Sacred places that bring cause for a shrine to be built.

- Places that become sacred because a shrine exists there.

ASTROLOGY

Astrology played a large part in Gupta medieval times. The person that read the stars for the family was typically the family priest who set important dates (e.g. journeys, weddings).

- More luck was believed for a child whose name shared the first letter of the stars.

- Horoscopes were read before a betrothal (pre-arranged marriage) took place.

THE COW

Hindus believe the cow is holy (killing them is regarded as a capital offense). Cows receive a season of the year where they are decorated with garlands and anointed with oil.

HOLY PERSONS

Brahmins are considered the most holy of people in the caste system.

- The most highly honored Brahmins are the **gurus**.
  - o Gurus teach Hindus religious principles that relate closely to their home lives. Not all gurus are Brahmins (but most are).
- **Sannyasins** are followers of Shiva (smeared in ash).
- **Sadhu** is a person that is at spiritual unity with the ultimate as they have had a samadhi (trance).

- o Easily identified by begging bowl, staff, and physical markings.
- **Yogins** are those that practice yoga in hopes of becoming sadhus or sanyasins.

PRACTICES

All stages of Hindu life include ancient religious practices such as:

- **Ayurveda** (Hindu medicine and healing (still popular today in the west)).

- **Hatha Yoga** (meditation)

- **Kundalini Yoga** (Tantric yoga focusing on waking the energy at the base of the spine making it rise through the seven charkas to the top of the spine).

- **Namaste** greeting (bringing palms together and a slight bow of the head which is a humble greeting).

- **Puja** (religious ritual that some Hindus perform every morning before eating (offering to a deity)).

- **Sadhu** (Holy Man) the choice to leave their homes to dedicate their lives to spirituality.

- Temples and Temple Rituals (building temples and the ceremonies that take place there).

LATER HINDUISM RELIGIOUS MOVEMENTS

Western religion and science has begun to influence Hinduism.

- Brahmo Samaj
  - o Founded in Calcutta 1828 by Ram Mohan Roy (Brahmin).
  - o Roy found all religion he studied (Buddhism, Zoroastrianism, Islam, Christianity) had similar core.
  - o Roy did not believe in multiple gods considering it idolatry.
  - o No pictures, images, or animal sacrifices are permitted.

- Discourages polygamy and child-marriage.
- Congregation style worship.
- Roy was still true to the caste rules.
- Another sect (Keshab Chandra Sen) developed with more emphasis on Christ and an attack on the caste system.

- Arya Samaj
  - A movement called"back to the Vedas".
  - Founded in 1875 by Swami Dayananda (a Brahmin).
  - Rejected the caste system.
  - Two branches are in existence (liberals and conservatives).

- Theosophy
  - Founded in 1878 in New York City but resides in India.
  - Establishes brotherhood among all people.
  - In the end, the world will drink from the Fountain of Wisdom and see that all religions have partial truths.
  - Believes in idol worship, caste, prophecy, and second sight.

- Ramakrishna Movement
  - Tolerant acceptance of western religions.
  - Ramakrishna was born a Brahmin and focused on Kali (the divine mother) and experiences samadhi (trance like state).
  - He tried many religions and found all gave him different paths to God.

- Secularism
  - Soft secularism
    - People can be identified apart from their religion.

- Hindu's find it difficult to identify themselves separately from their religion.
  - o Hard secularism
    - Less interest in organized religion
    - A turn away from religion

MAJOR HINDU HOLIDAYS

The major Hindu holidays are:

- **Mahashivarati** (also called **Shiva Ratri**)
  - o Most important to devotees of Shiva (but most Hindus celebrate).
  - o Day is spent meditation on Shiva, fasting, hymns, and offerings.
- **Holi (**also called **Holaka** or **Phagwa)**
  - o Least religious of all Hindu holidays.
  - o Friends gather and spray each other with colored powders and water.
  - o Celebration of the arrival of spring.
- **Diwali** (also called **Deepavali**)
  - o Hindu festival of lights that lasts five days.
  - o Also referred to as New Year's Eve.
  - o Celebrated with candles, lights, and fireworks.

SOCIAL REFORM FOR LATER HINDUISM

There has been much controversy with the caste and marriage laws that have far-reaching social consequences.

THE CASTE SYSTEM

The castes have broken into sub-castes (**Jati**) from the larger four-caste system (**varna**). People within a small Jati were only able to marry and socialize within this small group, greatly reducing the amount of people to form kinships with. The original caste system has multiplied into several thousand groups. For Hindus, karma justifies the caste system (i.e. the caste is deserved based on previous lives). The lowest castes are divided into two categories:

- The clean (**Shudra**)
    - Orthodox in religion.
    - Do not partake in occupations that degrade.

- The unclean (**outcastes, untouchables**)
    - Unclean occupations (cleaning the streets, preparing the dead).
    - Given separate drinking wells.

MARRIAGE AND WIDOWHOOD

Parents betrothed their young girls as young as a few months old, holding marriages before puberty. The idea was that a younger girl/bride would be easier to adjust to the new family's roles and responsibilities. However, in the event of becoming a widow the law prevents re-marriage and the widow becomes a permanent member/burden on the husband's family. Widowers could remarry, however that often led to middle aged men marrying young women (because older women were already married or an ineligible widow).

Part IV. Buddhism

This portion of your test will account for approximately ten percent of the questions. Part IV will cover:

- Historical development
- Major traditions
- Doctrine and practice

Historical Development

The creator of Buddhism was Prince Gautama Siddhartha (born in about 566 B.C.). He married a neighboring cousin, and after she had a son he left to pursue his religion. It was hard for people to understand why so fortunate a person would abandon household life, therefore to explain was the legend of the "Four Passing Sights".

The Four Passing Sights

The Four Passing Sights begins with the Prince's father knowing (from a soothsayer) that his son may give up all of his household fortunes to become a homeless monk. Therefore, to encourage his son to stay away from such a path and to pursue becoming a "universal monarch" his father insisted that he would shield his child from the unpleasant, and wouldn't allow him to know that people die. His father was so good at shielding the boy that the young prince didn't know that death, or hardships even existed. The gods decided they must intervene and the gods came to earth appearing in the shapes needed to show the prince the truth.

- A god came to him as a decrepit old man, thus the young prince learned what happens to people as they age.

- A god came to him as a diseased man, and the young prince learned of sickness and misery.

- A god came to him as a dead man, and the young prince learned of mortality.

- A god came to him as a calm **ascetic** (monk that renounces pleasures in life) in a yellow robe sitting under a tree, and the prince realized that true peace of soul would be life in a homeless state.

RENOUNCING THE HOME AND A SIX-YEAR QUEST

Despite his father's attempts to keep the prince in his home the prince was restless and left home to begin a six-year quest. In the six-years the young prince tried to follow Brahmin ways to test if they were the method to ultimate peace. He practiced:

- Philosophic meditation
    - Became the disciple of two **ascetic** (monk) teachers living in caves.
    - Practiced Yoga and meditation, and was disappointed.
- Bodily asceticism
    - Practiced for five years the act of self-deprivation, and self-harm to separate spirit and body.
    - He had five followers.
    - This period left him almost lifeless.

Neither method had brought him any closer to enlightenment, and when he abandoned asceticism the five followers left him as well.

ENLIGHTENMENT

Prince Gautama Siddhartha retired beneath a fig tree (Bodhi-tree, Bo-Tree) and became aware that his earthly desires (desire for life, love, etc) are the barrier to enlightenment. Only without any desires could Siddhartha become enlightened. Siddhartha also believed that he had lived the highest life he could, and this life would be his last. At this point Siddhartha became a Buddha and an **arahat** (a monk that had experienced enlightenment). Buddha had to decide if he would let his knowledge die with him as he returned to nirvana, or if he would share what he'd learned. He decided to share.

ASSEMBLING THE RELIGION AND THE CONVERTS

Buddha returned to the five ascetics who abandoned him and converted them creating the Buddhist monastic order (**Sangha**). The group traveled near and far gaining converts and a strong following. The recognition of the converts was simple (yellow robe, shaved head, beggars bowl, and daily meditation). The converts had to obey **Ten Precepts** (basically the Buddhist Commandments):

- Do not kill (**ahimsa**)
- Do not steal
- No sexual misconduct
- Do not lie
- No intoxicants
- Moderation in eating (no food after noon)
- Do not watch dancing, singing or other dramatics
- No garlands, perfumes, or other vanity articles
- No high or broad beds
- No silver or gold (no riches)

The Buddha recognized not all of these precepts would be obeyed by everyone who wanted to become Buddhist (for example, there were those who still wanted the household life). Therefore, some of the orders only had to obey the first five precepts.

Buddha later admitted a nun order and many of his family members became nuns (including his wife and stepmother) and monks (including his son) of Buddhism. However, the nuns were always beneath the monks.

BUDDHA'S PARINIRVANA AND BUDDHISM SPREAD

At the age of eighty the Buddha died among his followers beneath two trees. Soon after Buddha's death (**parinirvana**) five hundred monks met under the first council at Rajagrha (under Kashyapa's leadership). Buddha's lessons (**sutras**) were recited, committed to memory and the oral tradition of Buddhism lasted for over 200 years.

One hundred years later a second council was held in Vaishali where Buddhism split between the liberals and the traditionalists. The liberals became **Mahasangha**, and the traditionalists became **Sthaviravada** (way of elders). More disagreements continued eventually leading to eighteen different Buddhism schools of thought. Today only the Sri Lankan Theravadan school exists.

ASOKA

Asoka assumed the throne of Magadha and conquered most of India. However, Asoka became regretful of the warfare and suffering that he had caused and dedicated the rest of his life to one of peace. Asoka took his dedication to peace and Buddhism very seriously and to spread the word of his rules he issued 35 proclamations throughout his land. Including:

- "Fourteen Rock Edicts"

- "Seven Pillar Inscriptions"

- Two "Kalinga Edicts"

- Three "Cave Inscriptions"

- Four "Minor Pillar Edicts"

Asoka sent teachers of Buddhism to Sri Lanka, there all of the Sutras were recorded in the Pali language. These recordings are called **Theravada's Pali Canon** or **Triptaka** (three baskets). The three sections of it are:

- Monastic law (**Vinaya Pitaka**)

- Words of Buddha (**Sutta Pitaka**)

- Philosophy commentary (**Abhidamma Pitaka**)

CHINA

Buddhism was introduced to China with three competing religions (Confucianism, Taoism, and folk religion).Buddhism had stages of growth and repression based on which emperor was in power.

JAPAN

Japan embraced Pure Land (as it appealed to the peasant population), and later (in the 1200's) subscribed to the Zen practices. Finally, Japan embraced the **Nichiren School** (a nationalistic religion) that stressed only to pay homage to the Lotus Sutra.

TIBET

The early **"Red Hat"** sect (identified by the red they wore in lieu of the traditional yellow) survived significant persecution in Tibet during the ninth century. In the Tibetan culture the Buddhivistas (**upaya**) are coupled with female consort (**prajna**). The Tibetans use the prayer wheels, mandala, and mantras to express worship.

MAJOR TRADITIONS

Buddha did not believe that people would be saved through religious devotion. He believed that everything in the world was subject to the birth and death cycle with no eternal being. Therefore, Buddha rejected prayer and the Vedas.

MAJOR IDEAS

- **Three delusions** to life:
  - Ignorance
  - Desire
  - Anger/hatred
- **Three trainings** in Buddhism
  - Moral discipline
  - Concentration
  - Wisdom
- **Three marks** of existence
  - Impermanence (**anicca**)
  - Unsatisfactoriness (**dukkha**)
  - No-self (**anatta**)
- **Four reminders**
  - Equanimity (**upekkha**)
  - Loving-kindness (**metta**)
  - Compassion (**karuna**)
  - Sympathetic joy (**mudita**)
- **Four Bodhisattva vows**
  - Rescue the boundless living beings from suffering.
  - End to the infinite afflictions of living beings.
  - Learn the measureless Dharma-doors.
  - Realize the unsurpassed path of the Buddha.

- **Six Realms of Existence**
  - Hell-beings
  - Hungry ghosts
  - Animals
  - Humans
  - Anti-gods or demigods
  - Gods

KARMA

Buddhism still subscribes to the law of Karma with some variations from Hindu culture.

- Any person from any caste can experience a change of heart escalating him/her to a Buddha. There are no castes in the Buddha religion.
- People were made up of the union of five states of being (**skandhas**) that upon death disperse.
  - The body (**rupa**)
  - Perception (**jamjna**)
  - Feelings (**vedana**)
  - Instincts (**samskaras**)
  - Reason (**vijnana**)

THE THREE REFUGES

The Three Refuges (also called the Three Jewels, Three Treasures, or Triple Gem) are the three areas that Buddhists take refuge in and seek for guidance. They are:

- Buddha
- **Dharma** (teachings of Buddha)
- **Sangha** (the community of those that have attained enlightenment)

THE FOUR NOBLE TRUTHS

To resolve the issue with how one should live to attain freedom from the re-birth /re-death cycle was outlined in the four noble truths. The Four Noble Truths are:

- Suffering exists

- o Physical suffering (pain, sickness, etc)
- o Psychological suffering (sadness, fear, disappointment, etc.)
- Suffering is caused by attachment to our desires
  - o Craving and clinging to transient things causes our suffering.
  - o Family and friends cause suffering.
  - o The pursuit of material things causes suffering.
  - o Sense of self causes suffering.
- When our desires cease, as does our suffering
  - o The unmaking of sensual craving and attachment (**nirodha**) can cease suffering.
  - o By removing the cause of the suffering a person can overcome it.
  - o By being able to overcome all sense of suffering one can achieve **Nirvana** (freedom from all suffering and worries).
- By practicing the Eightfold Path we can be free from suffering
  - o A gradual path to self-improvement that can end suffering.
  - o Middle ground between **hedonism** (self-indulgence) and asceticism (self-mortification).
  - o Ends the cycle of rebirth.

THE EIGHTFOLD PATH

The Eightfold Path is a guide to lead the practitioner to be free from suffering and, combined with the Four Noble Truths, is the heart of Buddhism.

- Right View/Right Belief
  - o The belief in the Four Noble Truths
- Right Intention/Right Aspiration
  - o Resist the pull of desire

- o Resist anger and aversion
- o Harmlessness
- Right Speech
    - o No lies
    - o No slander
    - o No harsh words
    - o No idle chit chat
- Right Conduct/Right Action
    - o No harming self or others
    - o No theft
    - o No sexual misconduct
- Right Livelihood
    - o Choosing jobs that would be considered under the Right Speech and Right Conduct principles.
- Right Effort
    - o Intellectual awareness of distinguishing between wise and unwise desires.
- Right Mindfulness
    - o The ability to see things as they are through four foundations:
        - ▪ Contemplation of body
        - ▪ Contemplation of feeling
        - ▪ Contemplation of state of mind
        - ▪ Contemplation of phenomena
- Right Concentration
    - o Concentration on wholesome thoughts
    - o Rebirth will end forever

MAHAYANA BUDDHISM

In the Mahayana Buddhism there were three kinds of saviors:

- **Manushi Buddhas** (those that appear on earth, experience enlightenment, teach others, and return to Nirvana).

- **Bodhisattvas** beings that hear prayers and come to peoples aid. Benevolent beings that postpone their existence into Nirvana because of their compassion for humanity. Examples of Bodhisattvas that were worshiped are:
    - **Maitreya** (the Buddha after the original)
    - **Manjusri** said to assist those who want to know Buddhist Law (Dharma).
    - **Samantabhadra** brings happiness and kindness
    - **Avalokitesvara (Lord Avalokita)** god of compassion

- **Dhyani Buddhas (Tathagatas)** achieved their Buddhahood while in a non-earthly form and are the contemplative Buddhas. The most popular Dhyana Buddha is **Amitabha (Amida)** generally known as presiding over "the Pure Land" as he presides over the western heaven assuring future bliss.

Mahayana Buddhism was a middle approach to the religion and it split into two schools of thought, Yogachara and Tantra.

YOGACHARA (MIND ONLY)

Yogachara was a sect of Buddhism invented by Asanga and Vasubandhu in India. The Yogachara subscribed to the belief that the path to enlightenment was to meditate into pure consciousness making the mind devoid of any content.

TANTRA

Tantra is a sect of Buddhism that gives a basic guide to enlightenment. The optimum way to enlightenment was to study under a guru (not read it in texts) and learn the secret exercises that can help connect with reality. Some of the exercises were:

- Forming circles (**mandalas**) pictures providing a focus point for meditation.

- Reciting mantras.

- Casting hypnotic spells.

- Performing magical gestures (chanting, dancing, sexual union).

PURE LAND

Pure Land Buddhism spread to China and Japan. The motive of Pure Land was one that appealed to the common (to get to heaven). To get to heaven via the Pure Land method one must only have to have an unquestioning faith (in China it was referred to as the "easy path"). In Japan Pure Land was divided into the **Jodo-shu** (Pure Land sect) and **Jodo-Shinshu** (True Pure Land Sect).

MEDITATIVE SCHOOLS (CHAN AND ZEN)

The belief is that salvation or enlightenment is received by following meditation, as a personal experience. There are four conditions to the Chan/Zen sects:

- Oral transmission from master to disciple.

- No dependence on the authority of words.

- Direct pointing to the soul of man.

- Seeing into ones own nature.

RATIONAL SCHOOLS (TIAN-TAI)

The belief that meditation should be balanced with the study of the scriptures was the basis of the rational school. The Lotus of the Good Law was a favored text in the Tian-tai school. Three levels of truth were determined from the studying of scripture:

- All things are void

- All things are temporary

- All things are in existence and void at the same time

ESOTERIC/MYSTERY SCHOOLS (ZHEN-YAN AND SHINGON)

This school of thought was based on seeking enlightenment through the use of mandalas, genstures, and incantations. The followers performed their libations among firecrackers.

PART V. CONFUCIANISM

This portion of your test will account for approximately six percent of the questions. Part V will cover:

- Historical development
- Doctrine and practice

HISTORICAL DEVELOPMENT

Most of the information that we know about Confucius is through the *Analects* (the collection of sayings recorded by his disciples). Confucius was raised from humble beginnings (born in 551 B.C.), had an unsuccessful marriage (that resulted in a son), and his mother died while he was in his twenties. The details of Confucius' teaching are made available through the **Four Books**.

- The *Analects, Lun yu*
    - o Collection of sayings
- The *Great Learning, Da Xue*
    - o Serves as basis of education of gentlemen (Chinese education first text studied by boys).
- The *Doctrine of the Mean, Zhong Yong*
    - o Deals with human nature and the moral order of the universe.
- The *Book of Mencius*
    - o Collection of writings and sayings from the early Confucian followers

There were also what is referred to as the "**Five Classics**" (**Wu Jing**) that were written:

- Classic of History (speeches and writings from rulers) **"Shu Ching"**
- Classic of Odes (poems and songs) **"Shih Ching"**
- Classic of Changes (descriptions of divinity involving hexagrams, and telling the future with sticks) **"I Ching"**
- Spring and Autumn Annuals (history of the state of Lu from 722-484 B.C.) **"Ch'un Ch'iu"**
- Classic of Rites (group of three books) **"Li Ching"**

Doctrine and Practice

The main purpose of Confucianism is the principle of humaneness or benevolence with an optimistic view of human character. Confucius' ethical thought came from the idea that China was very corrupt, but not beyond salvation. His teachings stressed the following values:

- Li: Propriety (ritual and etiquette)
- Ren/Jen: Humane Character (benevolence, highest virtue to Confucius)
- Hsiao (love within the family)
- Yi (righteousness)
- Xin (honesty and trustworthiness)
- Chung (loyalty to the state)

Filial Piety: Xiau (Hsiao)

Confucius firmly believed in the obedience of a son to his father, even in death. The number one priority in Confucianism was to the family. Boys do not come of age, leave the nest, and create families of their own; sons are always tied to their original family and obedient to their father. Even upon a father's death the son will only do what his father would have approved of.

Social Philosophy

Confucius believed there is little to be done about the amount of time that we are given on this Earth, however man is responsible for what their accomplishments. The three main social doctrines of Confucius are:

- **Jen** (compassion) was a core concept in his social philosophy.
- **Superior man** (chun-tzu) practice benevolence regardless of family background.
- Ritual propriety means to act in accordance with propriety and conform to aesthetic norms.

Five Important Relationships

Confucius believed there were five important relationships to honor in life.

- Ruler to minister
- Father to son

- Husband to wife
- Older brother to Younger brother
- Friend to friend

POLITICAL PHILOSOPHY

Confucius traveled near and far to advise the rulers of Chinese governments. Confucius believed:

- Good character was the key to good leadership (possession of **de**).

- People should act in the social ideal of their place and function in the society of which they dwell.

- Superior Man (Jun-zi/Chun-tzu)

  o Obeys inner law of self control.

  o Acts with regard for others.

- Golden Mean (Zhongyong/Chungyung) nothing in excess.

CONFUCIANISM AND EDUCATION

Confucius did not believe in intuition or a natural understanding. He thought understanding was a direct result of finding a good teacher and long and careful study. His goal was to create gentlemen that acted with grace and integrity. He taught six arts; ritual, music, archery, chariot-riding, calligraphy, and computation.

TEACHERS AND CRITICS OF CONFUCIANISM

- Mencius (Meng Tzu)

  o Considered an orthodox teacher of Confucianism.

  o Based his teachings on **Jen** (benevolence and kindness).

  o Different than Confucius he believed if the leaders have failed to bring peace that the people have a right to revolt (social contract).

  o Believed that humans are innately good.

- Zhu Xi (Chu Hsi)

  o Most influential Neo-Confucian (rationalist).

  o Neo-Confucians included ideals from Buddhists and Taoists, but opposed Buddhism and Taoism.

- o Focused on the Four Books instead of the Book of Changes (as other Neo-Confucians did).
- o Least religious, held an agnostic attitude.
- o Believed that things were brought into being by union of Qi (physical force) and Li (rational principle).
  - Source of Li is Taiji (Great Ultimate)
  - Source of Qi is Ch'i

- Hsun Tzu (Xun Zi)
  - o Believed that man's tendencies need to be corrected through education and ritual (opposing Mencius' thought of man being innately good).
  - o Wrote Xunzi filled with elaborate essays that are critical of competing schools of thought (e.g. Taoism).

- Mo Tzu
  - o Despised Confucians (thought they were egotistical and pretentious).
  - o Believed that all humans were equal in the eyes of heaven.

CONFUCIANISM TODAY

Virtues that encourage social harmony and shared values are elaborated in the five ethical shared values of what Confucianists subscribe to today:

- Nation before community, society before self
- Family is the basic unit of society
- Respect for the individual
- Reach compromise, avoid conflict
- Racial and religious harmony

PART VI. TAOISM

This portion of your test will account for approximately four percent of the questions. Part VI will cover:

- Historical development
- Doctrine and practice

HISTORICAL DEVELOPMENT

The founder of **Taoism** (also called **Daoism**) was Lao-Tze (604-531 BCE) who was a contemporary of Confucius. He wrote a book *Tao-te-Ching/ Dao De Jing* that was a combination of psychology and philosophy, however ultimately Taoism became one of the three great religions of China. The *Tao-te-Ching is* often translated into English as the *Book of the Way*.

DOCTRINE AND PRACTICE

The Yin Yang symbol is one of the most recognized symbols of religion. The **Yin Yang** is a Taoist symbol that represents the balance of opposites throughout the universe. When they are equal there is a balance and serenity, however when they are not, there is chaos. The Yang is masculine (active, dry, bright, procreative), while the Yin is feminine (fertile, breeding, dark, cold, mysterious, wet).

THE PHILOSOPHY OF THE *DAO DE JING*

The *Dao De Jing* is the book outlining the philosophy of the religion. The *Dao De Jing* says when beings take their natural course they will find their own balance between Yin and Yang. There are several aspects of the *Dao De Jing* that may be important for the test:

- Non-Being
    - o People have the power to choose their own way (free-will) even against the Dao plans.
    - o To choose your own way without letting nature take its course will cause pain.

- Quietness
  - The Dao can only be felt through intuition.
- Low Position
  - The Dao is not aggressive, but still accomplishes all things.
- Reversion
  - People who don't follow the Dao way may actually succeed for a time, but will eventually return.
- One with nature
  - Become one with nature, don't try to master it (as the Westerns do).
- Spontaneity
  - Responding to the present moment naturally.

The *Dao De Jing* also lays out ethical conduct that is both positive and negative.

- Negative *Wu-Wei*
  - Do not meddle with nature as it takes its course.
  - Prefer what is natural.
- Positive *Wu-Wei*
  - Be attendant to human virtues (kindness, sincerity, humility).

DAOISM/TAOISM IN PRACTICE

The **Jade Emperor** is the Taoist ruler of heaven, man, and hell. He is the most prominent god in Taoism.

Daoism found a strong interest in preserving human life. Searches were held to search for the elixir of immortality. In order to prolong life and prevent the body from decay, the people began practicing a dietary and hygienic means of spiritualization. The ideal Taoist is the sage who lives in accordance with the Tao and knows that opposites are interdependent. The Taoist does not struggle, oppose, or strive and only intends to live within the natural course of things by practicing **wu-wei** (non-action). The Taoist hopes to seek longevity or immortality through many methods:

- Feng Shui
  - Based on **ch'i** (life energy) and the five elements.
  - Arrangement of color and location of items (for example in a home) will affect and redirect ch'i as needed.
- Breath control (**hsing-chi** and **t'ai-hsi**)
  - To keep the mind clear of tension.
  - Allows ch'i to permeate the body.
- Dietary restraints
  - Eating meat and the five cereals (rice, millet, wheat, barley, soybeans) poisons the body. Only live on fruits, berries, roots, and tubers.
- Sexual restraints
  - Similar to the Tantric Buddhist styles.
- Searching for the **Isles of the Blessed** where the Immortals live, to persuade them to share their secrets.

THE EIGHT IMMORTALS

The Eight Immortals are worshipped and sought after in hopes to find out their secret to immortality. They eat air, drink dew, and can fly. Frequently they appear in Chinese literature representing a special power.

- Li T'ieh-kuai
  - Represents the sick
  - Carries a gourd with magic healing potions
- Chungli
  - Represents military men
  - Wisps of hair, with a long beard and a fan
- Lan Tsiai-ho
  - Represents florists
  - Either a strolling, singing woman or a young boy in rags
- Chang Kuo-lao
  - Represents old men
  - Ruler with his mule
- Ho Hsien-ku
  - Female
  - Symbol is lotus blossom
- Lu Tung- pin
  - Represents barbers
  - Most widely known Immortal
- Han Hsian-tzu
  - Represents musicians
  - Peaceful mountain dweller
- Ts'ao Kuo-ch'iu
  - Represents actors
  - Connected with Sung Imperial family

Part VII. Judaism

This portion of your test will account for approximately sixteen percent of the questions. Part VII will cover:

- Historical development
- Denominations
- Doctrine and Practice

Historical Development

The origin of the biblical Hebrews (who spoke Semitic languages) is traced back to the Syro-Arabian desert where they wandered. Each group or tribe kept to itself under the rule of a single patriarch (**shaykh**). This group worshipped stones (**mazzebah**) and circular pillars (**gilgal**) with the idea that gods lived there. Trees and groves were considered spiritual even able to deliver oracles; however, trees were also feared because they could draw down the lightening of demons or hide an ambush of demons or beasts. For the early Semites snakes were feared and considered cunning. The wild animals in the forest were considered demon-gods (including the birds of prey). It came to pass that many of the most powerful spirits were given a universal name meaning divinity **eloah** (or **elohim**).

Eventually eloah (elohim) stood for one being. The relationship was one that resembled a chief to its people, or a child to its father. The Semantic people began to choose among the gods, which one would be their chief.

Abraham

In Genesis Abraham chose to worship the god El (he called him **El-Shaddai**). In choosing to worship him he listened to El Shaddai more intently than the household gods represented by wood or stone (**teraphim**). El Shaddai encouraged him to go to the southwest. Abraham and his family lived out their days in the land where the Canaanites dwelt. Abraham is known as the **patriarch** of Judaism.

Abraham's Descendants

A famine came to where Abraham's descendants lived, so they migrated to Egypt to the Land of Goshen where they lived for many generations. However, when Egypt fell under the rule of pharaoh Ramses II (1304-1237 B.C.E.) he turned them into slaves.

MOSES

Egyptian leadership worried about the multiplying of the Israelite men. Every son born of the Hebrews was to be killed. A woman from the House of Levi had a son (Moses) and hid him for three months. Once she could no longer hide him, she set him on some reeds in the Nile in hopes he would find someone to save him. The pharaoh's daughter came upon him and adopted him as her son.

Growing up Moses came upon an Egyptian beating an Israelite, and Moses killed the Egyptian. Moses fled to the land of Midian. In Midian he joined the Jethro household and married the priests daughter (having two sons with her).

THE BURNING BUSH

While Moses was tending a flock of sheep he came upon a bush that was on fire where he was commanded by God to deliver the people from Egypt to Sinai. In this scripture God calls Himself **Yahweh** (or also pronounced **Jehovah**). **Yahweh** can be translated a few ways; I will be what I want, I am who I am, or I am He that causes to be. Jews have found the word to holy for words; so instead, have said Lord, or Adonai.

THE PLAGUES OF EGYPT

Moses came to rescue his people and from God there were ten plagues of judgment on the people of Egypt. The ten plagues were:

- Water turned to blood
- Frogs
- Gnats
- Flies
- Livestock
- Boils
- Hail
- Locusts
- Darkness
- Death of every Egyptian firstborn

After Moses delivered the Israelites from Egypt (through the parting of the red sea) Moses was the instrument that God used to make a **covenant** (agreement) with the people.

Moses went up a hillside for several days and came down with two stone tablets with God's will for the people (the Ten Commandments).

The Ten Commandments are:

- No false idols
- Do not take the Lord name in vain
- Observe the day of rest on the Sabbath
- Honor your father and mother
- Do not kill
- Do not commit adultery
- Do not steal
- Do not lie
- Do not covet your neighbor's wife
- Love your neighbor as yourself

Ultimately Moses is largely credited with the Jews abandoning many gods (**polytheism**) for the one God (**monotheism**).

EARLY RITUALS

The earliest of rituals for the Jews are Passover and Sabbath.

THE PASSOVER

Passover is a Semitic festival celebrated during the spring equinox. Between twilight and dawn each family cooked a sacrificial goat or sheep (its blood smeared on the door posts to the house). The people or the fire must consume everything of the animal. Passover is a celebration of the Exodus.

SABBATH

One day of every moon was to be taken for worship and recreation. The custom morphed to become the seventh day of the week as the day of rest and worship of the Lord.

After wandering for 40 years, the Israelites (or **exodus-Hebrews**) were strong enough to invade Canaan. It took the Israelites a very long time to dominate Canaan,which they also had to defend against Edomites, Moabites, Ammonites, and the Philistines (non-Semitic pirates).

As the Canaanites and the Israelites merged cultures their religions became intertwined. The Canaanites worshipped farm gods known as **baal**. However, all the lesser baals fell under the two supreme ones:

- **El**
  - Elevated but inactive
  - Consort with **Ashirat** (Hebrew **Asherah**)
- **Baal of Heaven**
  - God of all the other baals
  - Storm god
  - Associated with his sister **Anath**, and virgin fertility baal **Astarte**

There were places of worship for these farm gods throughout the land, and each city built a sanctuary for their guardian baal (**bamoth**). Sacrifices of first fruits or animal flesh burnt at the altar were offered to these gods.

Because farming was new to the Israelites, when they learned it from the Canaanites they also learned the gods and rituals associated with farming. Many of the farming Israelites performed the same rituals and honored festivals of the Canaanites.

THE HEBREW PROPHETS

Israelite prophets began to speak of the future and God's will, however they were contradictory and many.

ELIJAH

He was a prophet against turning Yahweh into a nature religion with baals. He lived in the north when King Ahab was being convinced by his wife Jezebel to make the baal religion dominant. When Jezebel planned to have Naboth stoned so the king could have his vineyard Elijah stood in the vineyard and cursed the king.

The king retreated and fasted in fear. Elijah was said to have disappeared, and Elisha (a disciple) continued his work.

ELISHA

Elisha encouraged Jehu (a violent man) to start a revolution. Jehu annihilated the royal house and destroyed all things related to the baal tradition. While this didn't totally eradicate the tradition, Yahweh's superiority was never doubted again.

AMOS

Amos was the first of the literary prophets whose words were recorded. Amos prophesized that social injustice violated the covenant of brotherhood and the social sins would be punished.

HOSEA

Hosea was a literary prophet who likened his domestic trials to the Lord. Hosea had an unfaithful wife as the Lord had followers that weren't faithful. However, the important concept is that they loved and forgave anyway.

ISAIAH

Isaiah was an active prophet for almost forty years advising Judean kings. His faith was unshakable in Yahweh. Isaiah did not believe in the ritualistic ways of worship.

MICAH

Micah was the last prophet for seventy years. He prophesized against the prophets who succumbed to popularity, and discussed the essence of spiritual religion.

JERUSALEM

The priestly functions centralized in Jerusalem. By the removal of rural priests the religion became less intimate for those that lived far away from Jerusalem. Jeremiah reintroduced the idea that each individual can have a relationship with God, and the individual was individually responsible for his or her deeds.

EXILE

In 586 B.C.E. King Zedekiah rebelled against Babylon. Babylon's king seized Jerusalem destroying all of the buildings and the

Temple. He captured the king and made him witness the execution of his sons and had his eyes put out.

Almost everyone was taken out of the city, the national heritage was shaken so much that after this invasion, the people were referred to as Judeans or Jews (no longer Hebrews).

THE SYNAGOGUE

Jerusalem lay in ruins; therefore the holy place to worship was gone. The faithful began to meet in homes on Sabbath to read the scrolls of the Torah, writing of prophets, and prayers. Traditions were written, and copies were made of the ancient texts so the ancestors would not forget the beliefs in God.

THE JEWS AND HELLENISTIC INFLUENCE

The Greeks under Alexander the Great (332 B.C.E.) began expanding toward Egypt. The Greek culture began to influence the Jews everyday lives. The Rabbi's and the Book of Daniel was resistant to the Hellenistic religion.

When the power switched hands to Antiochus Epiphanes (King of Syria) he tried to force the Jews to worship Greek gods. He turned the Jewish holy places into places of worship for Greek gods, and made observing Jewish religion punishable by death. The priest Mattathias and his five sons (the Maccabees) revolted and with the help of the faithful Jews and restored all holy places.

JERUSALEM'S FALL

Among quarrelling Jews King Nero sent his son, Titus, to subdue the them. Titus pleaded with the Jews to surrender, which they did not. After a bloody battle where Titus executed many Jews through crucifixion Titus prevailed and many died.

BAR KOCHBA

Sixty years after Jerusalem's fall the Emperor Hadrian ordered the temple be rebuilt for Jupiter Capitolinus. Judea revolted and Bar Kochba (a military leader) led a battle to liberate. The Emperor responded by banning Sabbath, circumcision, and the study of the Torah.

After three and a half years the Roman's won the battle and turned the area into a province (banning Jewish people to enter). The Temple was rededicated to Jupiter, and only on the anniversary of its destruction were Jewish people allowed to enter. On the anniversary the Jewish people could enter and touch the original foundation of the original Temple to lament their nation (**Wailing Wall**). In 1967, due to an Israeli victory the western wall is in Jewish control.

DENOMINATIONS

HISTORIC JEWISH GROUPS

SADDUCEES

This group was a wealthy aristocratic group of priests that believed the Torah should be interpreted literally. They rejected the ideas of angels, apocalypse, and resurrection in the afterlife. Society-wise they did not rock the boat and let Hellenistic influence them, however their religious beliefs were unwavering.

PHARISEES

The Pharisees had no interest in the Greek influence, and their only interest was the Jewish religion. As opposed to the Sadducees the Pharisees believed the Torah had to be continuously interpreted for application in everyday lives. The oral tradition that accompanied the Torah was considered just as sacred as the Torah itself. A serious group, the Pharisees believed in a life of continuous prayer, and spiritual growth.

HERODIANS

Called the Herodians because they served the house of Herod. They were not harsh to the Greco-Roman culture, however they wanted to rule their own land no matter what.

ZEALOTS

The Zealots were passionate about getting Palestine out from under Roman rule. They lived in Galilee. The Zealots believed that rebellion would hasten the Messiah's arrival, and at times believed the Messiah was among them (one of their own).

ESSENES

Essenes withdrew completely from society and lived in Palestine waiting on the Messiah's arrival. They fasted, prayed, ate together, washed frequently, observed Sabbath, and were a nonviolent group. They practiced baptism and confession, and called themselves followers of "the way".

CURRENT JEWISH DENOMINATIONS

While the historic Jewish groups were in response to Rome's influence on Israel, the current denominations reflect the European and American influence on Judaism.

ORTHODOX JUDAISM

Orthodox Jews believe the entire Torah (both written and oral), and it all remains applicable to modern life. They recognize other denominations of the Jewish faith, but typically don't accept non-Orthodox marriages, divorces, or conversions because they were not performed in accordance with Orthodox Jewish law. The Orthodox Union certifies foods as Kosher around the world, the symbol a U inside a circle.

REFORM JUDAISM

Reform is the most liberal denomination in Judaism. Reform Jews are more inclusive of other movements. Some specific differences are:

- Women can be rabbis
- Interfaith marriages are recognized
- Gay and lesbians are welcome
- Lack of adherence to the dietary laws

CONSERVATIVE JUDAISM

Somewhere between Reform and Orthodox is Conservative Judaism. Conservative Judaism is founded by the teachings of Zacharias Frankel (1801-1875). Conservatives believe:

- Halakha (Jewish Law) should be adhered to in daily lives
- Keep Sabbath (Shabbat)
- Keep kosher (kashrut)
- Pray three times a day
- Celebrate Jewish holidays

Hasidic is a mystical Jewish movement that came from Germany. It believes in personal experiences with God over ritual and religious education. Hasidic Jew's religious leader is called a **rebbe** or **tzaddik** (may or may not be a rabbi). The rebbe is counseled on many matters of life (such as picking a spouse and buying a home), and their advice is authoritative. **Kabbalah** (Jewish mysticism) heavily influenced the Hasidic movement.

FIXING THE CANON

The Jabneh scholars had to figure out which of the writings were to be included in the Hebrew Canon, and which were not. They examined writings of three types:

- The **Torah** (basic literature describing the covenant), consisting of five books
    - Genesis
    - Exodus
    - Leviticus
    - Numbers
    - Deuteronomy
- The **Nebi'im** (writings of the prophets), there were three types of books
    - The historical books that told of pre-literary prophets (Joshua, Judges, I and II Samuel, and I and II Kings).
    - Writings of prophets that left a literary legacy (Isaiah, Jeremiah, Ezekiel).
    - Briefer writings of prophets (Hosea, Joel, Obadiah, Jonah, Micah, Nahum, Habakkuk, Zephaniah, Haggai, Zechariah, Malachi).
- **Kethubim** (other miscellaneous writinsg) including:
    - I and II Chronicles, Ezrah, Nehemiah, Psalms, Proverbs, Job, Ruth, Lamentations, Daniel, Ecclesiastes, The Song of Songs, and Esther

The result of what has been included is considered the "fixed canon", and what Christians refer to as the Old Testament. The

Roman Catholic Church acquired the books that were excluded later, and most of them were adopted into its own canon.

TALMUD

The Talmud is a major literary work by Rabbinic Judaism that discusses laws and his second only to the **Tanakh** (Jewish Bible). It is comprised of two parts:

- The **Mishnah** is a book that presents cases that were brought to judgment and were ruled on by a rabbi based on the Mitzvot (law) and spirit of the Torah.

- The **Gemara** is the part of the Talmud that has analysis of the Mishnah.

HOLOCAUST (SHOAH)

The Holocaust was the deliberate extermination of Jews by Nazi Germany under Adolf Hitler during World War II. The genocide of Jews was accomplished in stages:

- Legislation to remove Jews from society.

- Ghettos to physically separate them.

- Concentration camps to work Jews until they died of exhaustion.

- Extermination camps used to kill masses of Jews.

The Holocaust had a lasting impact on Jewish tradition. Since the Holocaust Jewish people can no longer be given martyrdom no matter how significant their sacrifice.

DOCTRINE AND PRACTICE

MAJOR HOLIDAYS

PASSOVER (PESACH)

Passover is a spring festival where Jews celebrate their release from Egypt. Nothing leavened can be eaten this week, and at the eve of the first day the Seder Feast begins.

At the **Seder Feast** a booklet containing a narrative is read throughout the ceremony, and after the first cup of wine the male head of house acts as the priest. Parsley is dipped in salt water and eaten to remember captivity, and then there is more wine, and the eating of bitter herbs. Throughout the feast the tale of the Exodus continues so the oral tradition is passed on.

Psalms are sung and the evening meal is served, a door is opened to invite the precursor of the Messiah (Elijah) in for a drink from the Elijah cup. The service ends with a psalm of prayer, and rejoicing ensues. For forty-nine days after the Seder feast (except during the new moon) there are no joyous occasions (including marriages) permitted. On the fiftieth day the **Shebhuoth** (Feast of Weeks – in the New Testament this is called the Pentecost) is a celebration of the first fruits of spring.

ROSH HASHANAH

Rosh Hashanah is the Jewish New Year (celebrated typically in September). The Talmud calls Rosh Hashanah the Day of Judgment. After the Day of Judgment are the Days of Repentance, and on the tenth day is **Yom Kippur** (Day of Atonement). Yom Kippur is a solemn holiday where Jews focus on atonement and reconciliation, and a rededication to following God's will.

SUCCOTH

Five days after Yom Kippur comes Succoth. Succoth is an eight-day thanksgiving festival (Feast of Booths, Tabernacles). The synagogues are typically decorated with fruits and flowers.

HANUKKAH

Also called the Feast of Lights, Hanukkah is celebrated for eight days in December. Hanukkah commemorates the rededication of the Temple by Judas Maccabeuse in 165 B.C.E.

PURIM

Purim is also called the Feast of Lots and is associated with the biblical book Esther. Gifts are exchanged within the family, friends, and sent to the poor. This is a joyous celebration with dancing and singing.

SHABBAT: THE SABBATH

Jews may not work on the Sabbath; it is a day for relaxation, study, and reflection. The Torah dictates the Sabbath as a day to remember God's creation of the world and saving them from slavery in Egypt.

- No Work
  - Including cooking, washing clothes, constructing, repairing, writing, making a fire, cutting, and fishing (39 categories in all).
- Encourage play
  - Reading, singing, strolling, and playing games are all encouraged on the Sabbath.
- Sabbath begins at sunset on Friday and lasts until sunset on Saturday.
- Sabbath preparation
  - Cleaning the house
  - Preparing a meal
  - Dressing nicely
  - Shortly after sundown the woman lights two candles to welcome Sabbath and a blessing is said.
- Sabbath meal
  - Family gathers for blessings.
  - Four blessings
    - Father blesses children
    - Husband blesses wife
    - Wine blessing (**Shabbat Kiddush**)
    - Bread blessing (**Motzi**)
- Closing Sabbath
  - **Havdalah** (separation) ceremony
    - Blessing wine
    - Smelling spices
    - Lighting and blessing candle

DAYS OF AWE

From the beginning of Rosh Hashanah to the end of Yom Kippur are the Days of Awe (ten days). These days focus on atonement, introspection, and repentance. During these days Jews believe that

God decides each person's fate for that year, it can be changed until Yom Kippur, after which the books are sealed.

YOM KIPPUR

Yom Kippur is the last chance to change the fate God has in store for you for the year. It is an intensive day of introspection and atonement. It is considered a time of seeking and giving forgiveness from sins against one another. During Yom Kippur Jews abstain from:

- Work
- Food
- Drink (even water)
- Sex

PRACTICES

Jewish ritual and practices are stated in Jewish Law (**halakhah**). Halakhah governs religious and daily life.

THE MITZVOT (COMMANDMENTS)

There are 613 individual commandments (**taryag mitzvot**). Rabbis can also institute rules that must be adhered to. There are three types of laws that rabbis create:

- **Gezeirah** – is a rabbinic law that is instituted to prevent unintentional breaking of the mitzvoth.

- **Takkanah** – a law that does not come from the Torah.

- **Minhag** – custom that has evolved enough to become a part of religious practice.

JEWISH WORSHIP AND PRAYER

Typical prayers are in the form of recitations found in the **siddur** (traditional prayer book). Jews are expected to pray three times a day (more on religious holidays). The ideal way to pray is with a **minyan** (ten adult males).

KEEPING KOSHER: JEWISH DIETARY LAWS (KASHRUT)

Kosher foods are outlined in Deuteronomy and Leviticus with specific instructions on what is considered edible. Non-kosher foods are called **trayf**.

- Fruits, vegetables, and grains are allowed
  - Exception is grape products (only wine and grape juice that is made under Jewish supervision is considered kosher).
- Animal that chew their cud and have cloven hooves are kosher.
  - Cow, sheep, lamb, goats, and deer can be eaten.
  - Pigs, rodents, and camels cannot.
- Animals that are to be eaten must have no disease or flaws (a post-mortem examination is done to verify).
- The animal must be slaughtered in a certain way to rid the animal of as much blood as possible (according to the Torah blood cannot be eaten).
- Certain parts of the animal are not kosher (sciatic nerve, fat surrounding the organs).

- Only domesticated birds can be eaten.
- Seafood with fins and scales can be eaten (no shellfish).
- Insects are not kosher.
- Meat (except fish) and dairy cannot be combined or eaten at the same meal.

There are several symbols on foods that indicate when the food can be eaten.

- K
    - Indicates the manufacture identifies the product as kosher.
    - Any product can carry this symbol (so Jews are wary of it).
- U
    - Indicates the Union of Orthodox Jewish Congregations identifies the product as kosher.
- P
    - Food is fit for Passover.
- M
    - Meat product
- D
    - Dairy product

LIFE CYCLE RITUALS

There are several rituals throughout the life of a person that are honored and celebrated in Judaism.

- Birthing and naming ceremony
    - First Sabbath after a Jewish child is born.
    - Father goes to synagogue and asks blessings for mother and child.
        - If girl, she is named.
        - If boy, he is named during the circumcision ceremony.
    - Jews outside of Israel are usually given a civic name and a Hebrew name that is used for religious ceremony.
- Circumcision
    - Performed on the eighth day of a boy's life.
    - Ritual takes place in the family's home.
    - Performed by **mohel** (properly trained Jew).
    - Sign of the covenant with God.

- Redemption of the firstborn (Pidyon Ha-Ben)
  - Firstborn sons devotion of life to service in the temple (however money can be paid to the priestly family to absolve them of this service).
  - Children that can become a part of the redemption ritual are:
    - First born sons (cannot come after the birth of any other child or miscarriage).
    - Not delivered by caesarean.
  - Takes place on 31st day after birth.
  - The kohein asks if the father would prefer to redeem child for five shekels and the father passes the coins to the kohein.
- Coming of Age (Bar and Bat Mitzvah)
  - Boys at 13 and girls at 12 are considered an adult under Jewish law.
  - After coming of age the child must adhere to the commandments, can lead religious services, and can count toward **minyan** (quota of ten adults for prayer).
- Jewish Marriage
  - Rabbis must be married.
  - First ceremony is betrothal (**kiddushin**).
    - Bride circles groom and wine is blessed
    - Rings are exchanged
  - Wedding ceremony
    - Couple stand under canopy (**chuppah**)
    - Couple recites seven marriage benedictions and share a glass of wine
    - Groom breaks wine glass under his foot
    - After the ceremony couple goes to private room to symbolize consummation of marriage (for a few minutes) then join festivities.
- Divorce
  - Considered tragic but allowed.
  - Husband and wife are interviewed to verify mutual consent anda **get** (divorce decree) is issued.
- Death Rituals (**Chevra Kaddisha**)
  - Eyes are closed and body is covered and laid on floor with candles lit next to it.

- Body is never left alone, there are **shomerim** (guards).
- No cremation, open casket, or embalming and burial as soon as possible.

- Mourning
  - Mourning is an extensive process.
  - When first hearing of the death the relative will tear their clothing and wear it for the first seven days and mirrors are covered (**shiva/shivah**).
  - During time between death and burial (**aninut**) family grieves privately and preparation for burial is their sole responsibility.
  - Final mourning (**avelut**) lasts for twelve months from burial for a parent only. During this time the mourner does not go to any celebrations.

PART VIII. CHRISTIANITY

This portion of your test will account for approximately eighteen percent of the questions (the heaviest emphasis on your test is this area). Part VIII will cover:

- Historical development
- Major traditions
- Doctrine and Practice

HISTORICAL DEVELOPMENT

Jesus of Nazareth founded Christianity in 33 A.D.. Jesus was born in a land where the Jews and Romans (Palestine was under Roman rule) were divided. Herod the Great died about the time of Jesus' birth. Herod the Great willed Palestine to be divided among his three sons. Jews quarreled within their own groups and against any Roman who tried to force Roman religion upon them.

There is little known of Jesus' early life, at about thirty years old, Jesus met a desert prophet (John the Baptist). John the Baptist traveled throughout Palestine to warn of the end of the world and to urge those to repent for their sins. Many followed him, repenting and being baptized in the river. As Jesus was baptized it was said that the Heaven's opened and God spoke. John the Baptist was later captured and beheaded. Jesus went to the wilderness to ponder his path and for forty days was tempted by sin.

At about the same time as John the Baptist was arrested Jesus proclaimed himself the Messiah and urged those to repent their sins. Four disciples (fishermen) immediately followed:

- Simon Peter
- Andrew (Simon Peter's brother)
- James
- John (James' brother)

Jesus preached to the surrounding towns, marketplaces, and fields. When it was discovered that Jesus had healing power he was sought from every locale.

THE TWELVE APOSTLES

The Twelve Apostles were Jesus' inner circle of disciples that were hand chosen by Jesus. The Twelve are:

- Simon (a.k.a Peter)
  - Brother of Andrew
  - Fishermen from Sea of Galilee
- Andrew
  - Brought people to Jesus (including his brother Peter)
- James
  - Older brother of John (first of the twelve martyred)
- John
- Philip

  - Eventually martyred

- Bartholomew
  - Witnessed the Ascension of Jesus
- Thomas (aka Didymus)
  - Nicknamed "doubting Thomas"
- Matthew
  - Former tax collector, became a prominent apostle
- Thaddaeus
- Simon the Zealot
- Judas Iscariot
  - The traitor
- Matthias
  - Chosen by the other apostles after Judas became a traitor to round out the twelve.

JESUS' TEACHINGS

Jesus preached near and far spreading the word of God's will. His teachings included:

- The end of an era was upon them
  - Those that repented would be admitted into heaven.
  - People living sinful lives that repented would be more worthy than those who felt no need to repent.
- Relationship to God
  - Pursue a relationship with God, not just a passing morning/evening prayer.
- Defining God
  - Forgiving, merciful, morally perfect, stern, righteous, and practiced perfect justice.
- God in nature
  - God works behind and through nature.
- Goodness of the body
  - The body is not a burden that you shed upon death.
  - Race is unimportant.
- Morality above ceremony
- Alternatives to retaliation

THE LAST SUPPER

Jesus foresaw his death and that Judas would betray him. During the Last Supper He broke bread and gave it to the twelve telling them that the bread was His body, and the wine was His blood. Later in the Garden of Gethsemane Judas betrayed him.

During the hearings before the Sanhedrin and Pilate the prosecutor asked if Jesus was the Messiah. When Jesus confirmed he was convicted of blasphemy and sentenced to death.

THE CRUCIFIXION AND RESURRECTION

Jesus was turned over to the Roman soldiers for crucifixion, and was forsaken by all except the women who would not leave him. Even his disciples scattered except John. Peter denied his involvement with him when he was identified.

Jesus' body was removed from the cross to prevent it being up during Sabbath and it was put into an empty tomb, which was later found empty. About 120 disciples left Galilee and went to

Jerusalem where they assembled the Book of Acts. The apostles were the official leaders of this group.

JUDAIZERS AND HELLENISTS

Christianity formed two groups, the conservatives (Judaizers) and the liberals who were influenced by Greece (Hellenists). While they both believed in Christ there were significant differences between the two. Hellenists were less stern about the dietary restrictions and food, while Judaizers were stringent to the rules and regulations the Old Testament spelled out.

EMPEROR CONSTANTINE

In the early fourth century AD when the Emperor Constantine converted to Christianity the religion became legal, and persecution of Christians stopped. Christianity grew rapidly and became a powerful religion that would be dominant during the Middle Ages and Renaissance.

A major conflict in religion began with a dispute over Aryanism. **Aryanisms** believed that Christ was more than a man, but not God himself. To resolve the dispute Constantine called a meeting of the church (**Council of Nicea**). The Nicene Creed was created that condemned Aryanism and declared Jesus "one substance" with God. Another dispute about Christ's divine and human nature was resolved at the Council of Chalcedon.

RELIGIOUS FREEDOM

In the 17th century many Christians crossed the Atlantic to seek freedom from religious persecution, and find economic prosperity. There was no attempt in American to stifle religious beliefs (aside from a bit by the Puritan communities).

INQUISITIONS

The purpose of the Christian inquisitions was not to transform the person that was being punished, but to make an example of them so others were terrified into obedience. The Inquisition had jurisdiction over baptized members of the Church. There were four different inquisitions:

- Medieval Inquisition (1184- 1230s)

    o Pope Innocent IV authorized use of torture when investigating heresy.

- Spanish Inquisition (1478-1834)
  - Operated under royal authority (King Ferdinand II and Queen Isabella I)
  - Targeted converts to Christianity from Islam and Judaism.
- Portuguese Inquisition (1536-1821)
  - Originally religious, but expanded to book censorship, divination, witchcraft, and bigamy.
- Roman Inquisition (1542-1860)

MAJOR BRANCHES

For the first 1,000 years there were no different branches of Christianity. While there were definitely groups that separated, they were typically small, and if they weren't a part of the church, they were considered not Christian. All three branches have many similarities. They all believe in:

- Trinity

- Divinity of Christ

- Inspiration of the Bible

ROMAN CATHOLIC

In the beginning all Christians were considered Catholics, because there was no other church (Orthodox, or Protestant) to distinguish it. Catholicism is largely attributed to Saint Peter. Catholics beliefs differ from the Protestant and Orthodox on several significant items:

- Pope's special authority.

- Saints can intercede on behalf of a person.

- Concept of Purgatory (place to purify before entering Heaven).

- Doctrine of **transubstantiation** (the bread used in the Eucharist (Mass) actually becomes the body of Christ once blessed by a priest).

There are several unique practices of the Catholic religion:

- Formality

- Celebration of Eucharist (Mass) held more often (weekly)

- Observe seven sacraments (religious rituals) commanded by God

- Catholic monks and nuns take vows of poverty, chastity and devote themselves entirely to worship and the church. Monastic orders include:
  o Jesuits
  o Dominicans
  o Franciscans

- o Augustinians
- Catholic priests take vows of celibacy.
- Rosary beads in prayer.
- Veneration (honoring) of saints.
- Salvation through baptism.
- Priests are the mediators between God and man.

The most important office of the Catholic Church is that of the Pope (Supreme Pontiff, Bishop of Rome, Vicar of Christ, Servant of the Servants of God). The election of the Pope is not taken lightly there are many steps:

- Pope passes away
    - o Prefect of papal household (a cardinal) informs the Camerlengo (highest-ranking cardinal), who assume papal command.
    - o Between popes is called **sede vacante** (vacant seat).
    - o Camerlengo confirms death with ceremony:
        - Wraps on his head (gently) with silver mallet.
        - Calls pope birth name three times.
        - If no response, then he is pronounced dead.
    - o Camerlengo directs the issuance of the death certificate and removes the ceremonial ring (**Ring of the Fisherman**) worn by all popes.
        - Ring of the Fisherman is a ring bearing the likeness of Saint Peter casting a net from a boat encircled by the pope's name.
        - It is a symbol of authority and is destroyed.
    - o Prefect of the household tells the Dean of the College of Cardinals, and all cardinals come to the Vatican.
- Novemdiales and Pope's funeral
    - o College of Cardinals makes funeral arrangements and nine days of mourning begin (**Novemdiales**).
    - o Pope is dressed, coffin is sealed, and body is placed near the entrance of Saint Peter's Basilica.
    - o Buried in a tomb beneath Saint Peter's Basilica.
- Next Pope
    - o Between 15 and 20 days of the pope's death the sequestered cardinals meet in a secret meeting

(**conclave**) at the Sistine Chapel to begin the election process.

o   Any Catholic man in good standing can be elected (but since 1522 it has always been a cardinal).

o   The new pope takes a new name.

ORTHODOX (GREEK AND RUSSIAN)

In 1054 A.D. through the "Great Schism" the Western Church (Catholic) and Eastern Church separated. Pope Leo IX excommunicated the leaders of the Eastern Church (**Patriarch of Constantinople**), and the patriarch condemned the pope. The Eastern Church became known as the Greek Orthodox Church, while the west was the Catholic Church. The Orthodox is typically more abstract and mystical than the more literary and pragmatic Catholics. The break between the two religious beliefs came shortly after the death of Emperor Constantine who divided his kingdom between his two sons (west and east).

The Orthodox Church is organized into regions with **autocephalous** (each having a head bishop that governs themselves). While the Patriarch of Constantinople is the highest authority he doesn't have the same power as the Catholic Pope. The major divisions of the Orthodox churches are:

- Greek Orthodox
- Russian Orthodox
- Romanian Orthodox
- Bulgarian Orthodox
- Church of Alexandria
- Church of Jerusalem
- Orthodox Church in America

Orthodox Christians believe that humans were created in the image of God and sinning causes a barrier between God and man. The only repair to this barrier is salvation through death, which is made possible through Christ's death.

PROTESTANT

In the 16th century another movement (Protestant Reformation) occurred. Martin Luther and his 95 Theses sparked this branch.

Protestants emphasize the individual interpretation and relationship with God. As the Protestant movement spread it became many different denominations.

- Presbyterianism
    - Scotland under John Knox
- Anabaptists
    - Spiritual ancestors of today's Amish, Mennonites, Quakers, and Baptists.
    - Developed in Switzerland.
- Anglicanism
    - Established in 1534 under England's King Henry VIII.
    - Later became Episcopalian in America.
    - Methodism (teachings by John Wesley) also rooted in Anglicanism.

The Protestants differed from the Roman Catholic denomination on many topics:

- Rejected prayer to saints.
- Rejected the idea of Purgatory.
- Rejected the idea of transubstantiation.
- Scripture is the sole authority (rejected the idea of tradition an authority).
- Salvation is the result of divine grace and is unconditional.
- God will save regardless of church membership.
- No mediator necessary (priest) between God and man.

THE NEW TESTAMENT

The Hebrew Scriptures became known as the Old Testament, and the New Testament dealt with Christ's teachings and life. The last 27 books of the Bible are considered the New Testament. The New Testament is divided into:

- Gospels

- Acts of the Apostles

- Pauline Epistles

- Catholic or General Epistles

- Revelation

GOSPELS

The four gospels in the Bible are the narratives of Jesus' life. They are primarily proclamations of Jesus as the Messiah, and covers mainly his adult life to his death.

- Mark
    - o Based on the recollections of Saint Peter, it discusses Jesus' baptism, ministry, and Jesus' human feelings.
    - o Does not discuss Jesus' birth or time before baptism.
- Matthew and Luke
    - o Discusses the virgin birth, and the supernatural happenings of Jesus' youth.
    - o Discusses how to get to Heaven and Jesus' saving of humankind.
- Fourth Gospel (John)
    - o Identifies Jesus as The Word of God (Logos)
    - o It does not follow Jesus' life like Mark, Matthew, and Luke

ACTS OF THE APOSTLES

The Acts of the Apostles outlines the growth of Christianity after Christ's death. Some of the highlights to Acts of the Apostles are:

- Jesus' ascension to Heaven.

- Holy Spirit's arrival at Pentecost.

- Persecution of Christians (Christian martyrdom).

- Paul's missionaries in the Roman Empire.

- Peter's preaching.

PAULINE EPISTLES

The Apostle Paul wrote many of the books in the New Testament. The Pauline Epistles were written to churches that he had or was planning to visit. The Apostle Paul gave advice to churches and helped them with doctrine and moral matters.

CATHOLIC OR GENERAL EPISTLES

The Catholic or General Epistles are advice books but not written to a particular individual or church.

REVELATION

The Book of Revelation is the last and apocalyptic book in the New Testament. It includes prophecies that signify the end of the world.

MAJOR HOLIDAYS

EPIPHANY

Epiphany commemorates the presentation of Jesus to the **Magi** (three wise men). In religion an epiphany is the appearance of a divine being in visible form. Typically the Epiphany is celebrated on January sixth, and the time between Christmas and January sixth, is known as the Twelve Day.

LENT

Lent is a 40-day fasting period of repentance and reflection. In early days of Christianit, the congregation ate a single meal every day during this season (that is rarely observed today). Today, something of importance to the member is given up to show sacrifice and increase reflection of God.

MARDI GRAS

Mardi Gras (Fat Tuesday, Carnival, Shrove Tuesday) is the last day before Lent. Therefore, it is the day that all of the rich and fatty foods are eaten from the house in the form of a big party.

PALM SUNDAY

Palm Sunday (Passion Sunday, Willow Sunday, Flower Sunday) is the sixth Sunday of Lent and the last Sunday before Easter. Palm Sunday represents Jesus' entry into Jerusalem (the people laid palms in his path) where he would be crucified five days later. Ceremonies include:

- Blessing of palms
- Burning of palms to be used on Ash Wednesday
- Processions with palm branches

ASH WEDNESDAY

Ash Wednesday is the first day of Lent. Typically for Catholics the ashes of the palm are blessed, sprinkled with holy water and fumigated with incense. Crosses of ash are placed on the foreheads of all willing members of the congregation, for Catholics it is also a day of fasting.

GOOD FRIDAY

Good Friday is the day of Jesus' crucifixion; it is a day of fasting and penance.

EASTER

Easter is the most important holiday of the Christian faith. Easter commemorates the resurrection of Christ three days after his death. Lent (the 40 day fasting period) precedes Easter.

ADVENT

Advent is the beginning of the Church year. For the Western Churches it is near November 30 and in the Eastern Orthodox Churches it begins on or about November 15. It was typically a period of fasting and repentance as people prepared for Christ's second coming. However, today it is more of an anticipation of Christmas (i.e. the Advent Calendar).

Christmas is the celebration of the birth of Jesus. Some Christian denominations do not celebrate Christmas because birthdays aren't a celebration according to their beliefs.

SUNDAY

For Christians the day of worship is Sunday (as opposed to the Jewish Saturday) because the resurrection occurred on a Sunday.

PRACTICES

In general **Christians** practice:

- Baptism
- Confirmation
- Sunday services
- Prayer
- Bible Study
- Missions
- Ordination
- Marriage
- Healing
- Funerals

Distinctive **Protestant** rituals include:

- The Altar Call (Evangelical)
- Speaking in Tongues (Pentecostal)
- Spirit-Led Worship (Quaker)

Distinctive **Catholic** practices are:

- Mass
- Confession
- Penance
- Last Rites
- Veneration of the Saints
- Devotion to Mary

- Praying the Rosary

- Pilgrimages

- Stations of the Cross

  o The Fourteen Stations of the Cross refers to Jesus' final hours of life. Catholics typically hold mass during Good Friday (the first Friday of lent) to celebrate the Fourteen Stations of the Cross. The Fourteen stations are:

- Ordination to Religious Orders

- Monastic Life

- Holy Water

- Exorcism

TRINITY

Most Christians believe in the Holy Trinity. The Holy Trinity is the idea that there is one God that consists of three Persons. The Father (God), the Son (Jesus Christ), and the Holy Spirit make up the Trinity.

There are a few Christian faiths that do NOT share this belief:

- Aryanism (4th Century)

- Jehovah's Witnesses

- Mormons

- Unitarianists

The reasons some Christian groups don't believe in the Trinity are:

- Trinity is not mentioned in the bible.

- Philosophically unsound.

- Not the definition of monotheism.

The reasons that most Christian groups do believe in the Trinity are:

- It can be inferred in the Bible.

- Explains Jesus' divinity, while holding true to monotheism.

- The early councils that deemed the Trinity true are authoritative.

PART IX. ISLAM

This portion of your test will account for approximately sixteen percent of the. Part IX will cover:

- Historical development
- Major traditions
- Doctrine and Practice

HISTORICAL DEVELOPMENT

The religion for the Arab world before Islam was an animistic polytheism. The founder of Islam is Muhammad born in 570 AD in Mecca. At 40, he claimed to have seen the angel Gabriel. Gabriel's message was to convert from pagan polytheism and worship, Allah, the only one and true God. He and his followers suffered heavy persecution at first. However, in Yathrib they were in need of a strong leader, the people of the city vowed allegiance to Allah if Muhammad would lead their city. The escape of Muhammad to the city of Yathrib is celebrated through Hijira, and marks the beginning of the Muslim calendar in 622 AD. Today, Yathrib is known as the city of Medina.

MUHAMMAD'S SUCCESS

Muhammad succeeded as an able and strong leader for the city, and they began to have years of battle with his former city of Mecca. In 630 Muhammad's army defeated Mecca and rededicated the Ka'ba temple to Allah. Muhammad died in 632, and within 100 years of his death Islam had spread rapidly (largely due to the military and political abilities of his successors (**caliphs**)).

CALIPHS (632-661)

The first of four Caliphs was Muhammad's father-in-law Abu Bakr. Bakr was caliph from 632 to 634 and his major accomplishments were:

- Defeated a nomadic Arab (**Bedouins**) revolt known as **Ridda.**
- Set goals to expand Islam to the west in Europe, Syria, Egypt and the Mediterranean Sea, but died before being able to carry them out.

Another father-in-law of Muhammad, Umar, succeeded Bakr. His leadership lasted from 634-644. His major accomplishments were:

- Conquered Damascus in 635 and Jerusalem in 637.

- Instituted two taxes

  o **Kharah** (landowner tax for productive fields).

  o **Jizya** (non-Muslim paid tax for other religions right to practice).

- In Egypt, he defeated Babylon in 641 and Alexandria in 642.

Uthman, a member of an influential family (Umayyad) succeeded Umar after his assassination. Uthman served from 644-656. He was not a very popular leader with the Muslims he:

- Appointed members of his family to administrative positions.

- Spent a good portion of the money of the administration.

- Tried to create a definitive text of the Qur'an.

  o He succeeded, but not without controversy.

  o People thought he altered the sacred texts.

Egyptians assassinated Uthman in 656 and a fight over who would be the next caliph erupted. Ali declared himself the next caliph and Mu'awiya (Uthman's cousin) disagreed. Ali and Mu'awiya decided that a council could use the Qur'an to decide who was become the fourth caliph. The council said both should step down, and Ali refused. Ali was eventually killed and Mu'awiya became the fourth caliph.

MAJOR TRADITIONS

Islam do not have many holidays. Muslims celebrate two main festivals:

- Eid Al-Fitr
  - A three-day festival marking the end of Ramadan.
  - Prayers, worship, and gift exchange are common during this festival.
- Eid Al-Adha
  - Four-day festival celebrating God's gift to Abraham to sacrifice a ram in place of Isma'il (Ishmael).
  - Families that can afford to, sacrifice an animal and divide the meat among themselves, and their community.
  - Prayers, worship, and gift exchange are common during this festival.

There are also a couple of fasting times:

- Ramadan
  - Month of daytime fasting,
  - From dawn until dusk food, drink, and sex are not permitted.
  - At the end of the fast is the Islamic festival 'Id Al-Fitr
- Ashura
  - Day of Voluntary fasting
  - For Shiites this is a major festival, commemorating the death of Hussein, which is the event that led to the spit between the Sunni and Shia sects of Islam.
    - Some Shiites commemorate by public expressions of mourning and grief.
    - Passion plays depicting the death of Hussein are presented.

DOCTRINE AND PRACTICE

The **Qur'an** is the most holy book for Islam, and is considered a book of divine guidance for mankind. It is divided into **Suras** (or chapters). Islamics believe that the Quran was revealed to Muhammad through the Angel Gabriel (Jibril) from 610-632. While it primarily was oral, Muhammad's companions wrote it down, and the text was standardized in 653 (where it was produced in large numbers for the people).

PRACTICES

THE FIVE PILLARS OF ISLAM

All sects of the Muslim faith practice the Five Pillars of Islam. The **Five Pillars of Islam** are:

- Confession of faith (**shahada**)
    - Recitation of the confession of faith before two Muslims is required.
    - The confession accepts Allah and his prophet (Muhammad).
- Ritual prayer (**salat**)
    - Ritual prayer is done five times a day by a prayer leader (**imam**).
    - Prayer is directed toward the Ka'ba shrine in Mecca.
    - Ritual washing of face, hands, and feet (can be done with sand if no water is available) preceds salat.
    - Starting in a standing position the prayers move through several different postures.
- Alms tax (**zakat**)
    - Explicitly required by the Qur'an as a Muslim duty.
    - Rate is 2.5 percent of the value of all possessions.
    - Five categories of goods are subject to tax (grains, fruit, animals, gold and silver, and moveable goods).
    - The taxes are given to the poor, debtors, pilgrims, and tax collectors.

- o In Shi'a Islam an additional one-fifth tax (**khums**) is paid for orphans, poor, travelers, and imams.
- Fasting during Ramadan (**sawm**)
  - o All adult Muslims abstain from food, drink, and sex from sunrise to sunset.
  - o Increased prayer is expected during this time.
  - o The "Night of the Power" is considered the holiest night of the year during Ramadan.
- Pilgrimage to Mecca (**hajj**)
  - o At least once in a Muslims life they are expected to make a pilgrimage to Mecca during the last month of the Islamic year.
  - o If financially or physically unable, then they should not go, but can send someone in their place.
  - o When arriving into the Mecca boundaries people wear special garments and cannot hunt, fight, or have sex.
  - o The ritual includes
    - Walking around Ka'ba seven times (**tawaf** or **circumambulation**). Kissing or touching the black stone, praying twice toward Abraham, and running seven times between small mountains of Safa and Marwa.
    - Second stage is the 8th and 12th days of Dhu that begins with a sermon.
    - The tenth day is the Eid al-Adha (Feast of Sacrifice) where the pilgrim sacrifices and animal and throws seven small stones at the three pillars on three consecutive days.
    - The pilgrim then returns to Mecca to repeat the tawaf. Shaving the head, or trimming the hair completes the ritual.
    - Those that have made the pilgrimage can add Hajj or Hajji to their names.

MAJOR BELIEFS

SIX ARTICLES OF FAITH

Typically the Muslim doctrine (regardless of sect) is summarized in the **Six Articles of Faith**. The six articles of faith are:

- One God
- God's angels
- Books of God (specifically the Qur'an)
- Prophets of God (especially Muhammad)
- Judgment Day
- Supremacy of God's will

MUSLIMS AND GOD

Muslims believe in only one God (**Allah**). He is unique, perfect, fair, and indivisible. While God has revealed His will, His nature is unknown. Muslims also believe that God is merciful to those that cry out to Him. His gift of Muhammad the prophet was an example of his mercy.

MUSLIMS AND THE PROPHETS

There are five prophets that Muslims recognize:

- Noah
- Abraham
  - Muslims trace their ancestry back to Ishmael, the first-born son of Abraham.
  - Sarah (Abraham's wife) was barren, so Abraham took a second wife Hagar who bore Abraham Ishmael. However, Sarah then bore Isaac and because she fulfilled her duties she told Abraham he must reject Hagar and Ishmael (which he did).
  - Muslims believe that Isaac ancestors became the Jews and Ishmael's, the Muslims.
- Moses
- Jesus (considered a prophet, not the savior)
- Muhammad

- Muhammad is referred to as the "**Seal of the Prophets**" the last and greatest prophet of God.
- He is not divine.

MUSLIMS AND HUMAN NATURE

The Qur'an states that Allah created man from a clot of blood. Muslims believe in the original sin from Adam and Eve, but as Adam and Eve begged forgiveness Muslims differ from Christians and believe that people are born in a state of submission (**Al-Fitra**). Pride is a cardinal sin, while submission (or Islam) is considered the greatest virtue.

MUSLIMS LIFE AND SALVATION

Muslims believe that in order to achieve Paradise they must live a life that is pleasing to Allah. At puberty an "account" of each person's deeds is opened and it will be used to determine their fate at the Day of Judgment. Muslims believe that those that do not believe (**kuffar**) and sinners are condemned; however, genuine repentance will result in forgiveness and they will realize Paradise.

MUSLIMS AND AFTERLIFE

Muslims believe the soul lives on past death, and a Day of Judgment will decide the eternal destination (either Paradise or Hell) of each soul. The Qur'an also states that the world will be destroyed and Allah will raise all people to be judged, but until the Day of Judgment all souls stay in their graves awaiting resurrection. Those that are going to Hell will suffer in their graves, while those that are bound for Paradise will be at peace until the Day of Judgment.

- Day of Judgment
  - Depends on the deeds in life.
  - Pass over Hell on a narrow bridge to enter Paradise.
    - Those that fall (weighted by the sins) will stay in Hell forever.
  - There are two exceptions to the Day of Judgment:
    - Warriors that die fighting for God are immediately sent to Paradise.

- Enemies of Islam are sentenced to Hell immediately.

- Paradise
  - Also called the Garden (**Janna**) is full of spiritual and physical pleasure.

- Hell
  - Frequently mentioned in Qur'an.
  - Has seven doors with various levels, and the level depends on the degree of the offense.
  - Some believe because God is merciful that Hell will eventually be empty (as He can rescue those from Hell).

MUSLIMS AND RELIGIOUS TOLERANCE

Islamic sects are not technically denominations because the sects do not recognize members of other groups as Muslim, and conflict between sects is common.

DENOMINATIONS (SECTS)

AHMADIYYA

Established in 1889, by Mirza Ghulam Ahmad, it is mainly practiced in Pakistan. Ahmad claimed to be the promised Messiah, and upon his death Mawlawi Nur-ad-Din led them. When Din died the sect split into two:

- Quadiani
  - Those that recognized Ahmad as a prophet.
- Lahore
  - Those that recognized Ahmad as an Islam reformer.

SHI'A ISLAM

Shia Islam second in popularity only to the Sunnis. The split between the Sunnis and Shiites occurred when Muhammad died, those that followed Ali are known as the Shiites. Shiites are known for the "Twelvers" or Jafaryia (which refers to the number of Imams they recognize after Muhammad).

- The Imams
  - For Shiites the term means the leaders of the religion (for Shiites there were only twelve).
  - Shiites believe that the Twelfth Imam has never died or will re-manifest himself to become the Messiah.
- The various Shiite sects
  - **Zaidites** (Zaydis)
    - Disagree with other sects about the fifth Imam.
    - Most closely resemble the Sunnis.
    - Steers clear of the Imams beliefs.
    - They are nearly extinct today.
  - **Seveners** (Isma'ilites)
    - Believed that the Seventh Imam should have been Isma'il, but his father, because of rumors of drunkenness, set him aside.
  - **Twelvers** (Ithna 'Ashari)
    - Greatest majority of the Shiites.
    - Get their name from the Twelfth Imam, which they say vanished in 878, and will return on the day of reckoning.
- Shiites rituals
  - Observe the month of martyrdom.
  - Conduct pilgrimages to the shrines of the Twelve Imams.
  - Muharram passion plays, and major religious holiday.
    - Muharram was the Third Imam who was killed in 680.
- Shia Institutions
  - **Mosque** (all Muslims) religious center.

- o **Hoseiniyeh** (specific to Shiites) is a site for recitals celebrating the martyrdom of Husayn.

- o **Madraseh** (seminary) to advance the training of Shia leadership. Students (**talabehs**) stay for seven years and graduate as a low-level religious leaders (**mullah**).

- o **Maktabs,** or primary school, that is run by the clergy.

- o **Shrines** are scattered throughout Shiite territory and offer libraries, meals, and museums for those that visit.

- Shiite religious leaders (**ulama**)

  - o People that leave the madraseh after primary training can become prayer leaders, village mullahs, and other lowly religious positions.

  - o People that leave after completing the second level can become religious leaders in town and city mosques.

  - o **Mujtahids** are the highest religious authority. They are religious scholars.

    - In the twentieth century those mujtahid that attract many followers are called **ayatollah**. Some are considered **ayatollah ol ozma** (grand ayatollah).

KHARIJITES

Initially withdrew from Ali and were considered the separatists. They believed that the Muslim leader (caliph) should be elected upon merit, not their relation to the Prophet's family. They also believed that those Muslims that joined for political or economic reasons were not true Muslims and should be destroyed. This sect still exists (in a milder form) in Zanzibar and Algeria.

MURJITES

They opposed the Kharijites and believed that it was up to God not people to judge who is a Muslim.

Islamic mystics are Sufis, and grew from an ascetic movement (it first began between 661-749 during the Umayyad Dynasty). They have written significant poetry and hymns that focus on God's love for man.

- Sufi beliefs
    - o **Tawakkul** (absolute trust in God).
    - o **Tawhid** (there is no deity except God).
- Sufi practices
    - o Hope to attain **ikhlas** (absolute purity of intention and actions) through self-denial and introspection.
    - o Little sleep, talk, and food are fundamental to Sufism.
- **Tariqah** (Sufi path) ultimate goal is to fight the war against lower self (represented by a black dog).
    - o Repentance and to follow a guru (**sheikh or pir**).
    - o If accepted by the guru, then the prospective Sufi becomes a disciple (**murid**). The guru then prescribes lifestyle for asceticism and meditation (e.g. fasting, poverty, sexual abstinence).
    - o The mystic undergoes changing spiritual states and it culminates into a **mahabbah** (love).
    - o The final stage is annihilation (**fana**) one with God's love. After annihilation the mystic enters their "second sobriety" and continues to live according to God's rules.

SUNNI ISLAM

Sunni Islam is the largest sect of Muslims. They are known as Sunnis or Sunnites and are identified as those who followed Abu Bakr after Muhammad's death.

SHARI'AH (LAW)

In the law of Islam all actions are divided into five types:
- Obligatory
- Recommended

- Indifferent
- Repulsive
- Forbidden

Punishments are inflicted for neglecting obligatory actions, or performing forbidden ones. The middle three are a gray area where there is significant latitude to choose to inflict punishment.

Due to the ever-changing landscape of society, a group of religious scholars (**ulama**) interpret the **Shari'ah** (law).

- Hanifite
    - Founded by Abu Hanifa (died in 767).
    - Begin with Qu'ran and try to draw an analogy to a current situation (ignored the Hadith).
    - If the analogy didn't appear to the public good, then he consulted **ra'y** (reasoned justice) from the **istihsan**, and made a ruling.
    - These ruling supercede the Qu'ran when prescribed in the interest of the public good, most liberal.
- Malikite
    - Founded by Malik ibn Anas (715-795).
    - Interpreted laws with the Qu'ran and **Hadith** (collection of sayings by Prophet Muhammad) together.
    - Referenced the public opinion (**ijma**) for difficult decision.
    - He put together the hadiths of Medina, where he lived.
- Shafi'ite
    - Founded by al-Shafi'i (died 820)
    - Four roots of the law
        - Words of God (Qu'ran)
        - Words and deeds of the Prophet (as told in **Hadith**)
        - Muslim community opinion (**ijma**)
        - Analogies by jurists (**qiyas**) brought about by reasoning.
- Hanbalite
    - Founded by Ibn-Hanbal (died in 855) and is the most conservative of all schools.
    - Adhered to the letter of the Qu'ran with only supplementary reliance upon the Hadith.

Because this is a study guide, some of these words are found throughout the text, however there are some new ones, be sure you understand the meanings to all of these words because they will help you exponentially during the multiple choice test… Remember what you can, make flashcards for the rest, and quiz yourself a lot, you won't regret it!

Abhidharma pitaka - higher teachings

Acolyte – lay person who assists ministers in services (Christian)

Acupuncture - Chinese medical treatment using needles to stimulate the flow of ch'i in the body

Adhan – a way of calling Muslims to the five obligatory daily prayers

Adi-Buddha –the one source of the five celestial Buddhas (north, south, east, west, center)

Adonai – one of the Jewish names for God, typically used in prayer

Adoptionism – the teaching that Jesus was actually a human who was adopted by God (idea brought by Elipandus Archbishop of Toledo and Felix Bishop of Urgel)

Advaita – non-dualism, in Hindu philosophy the denial of the duality of the self and the world

Aeneas – Hero of Greek mythology, son of Anchises and the goddess Aphrodite (in Iliad he is a Trojan pious Trojan leader)

Agape - gathering of Christians for a common meal (love feast)

Agama – Hindu scripture

Aggadah – stories, legends, theologies in the Talmud and Midrash

Agni – sacred fire and the ritual priest of fire and light

Agnostic – neither the belief nor disbelief in a god

Agora – large open space used for Greek assemblies

Alexandrian School – Christian school that believed in the divinity of Christ over the humanity of Christ

Aleinu – Jewish closing prayer of service proclaiming God's sovereignty

Aliyah – Jewish being called up to recite blessing before Torah reading

'Am ha' aretz – common folk (distinguished from religious observers, pious people)

Amaterasu – sun goddess of Shintoism

Amida – focus of devotion for Pure Land Buddhism celestial Buddha that vowed to lead all beings to Pure Land

Amish (Amish Mennonites) – Conservative Christian group created by Jakob Amman (1656-1730) that migrated to North America

Amitabha – (Amida) Buddha of the west "Pure Land"

Amudah – desk in synagogue where Torah is read (Jewish)

Analogy – comparing something sacred with something ordinary

Ananda – meaning bliss, Buddha's cousin, memorized and recited all Buddha's teaching

Anathema – Christian cut off from the church, more serious than excommunication

Anicca – the fact that al things are temporary

Animism – the belief that all nature is filled with spirits (common for the oral religions)

Annitya (anicca) - change, impermanence of all things

Anthesteria – Athenian festival to god Dionysus to celebrate spring and wine maturation

Antiminsion (antimension) – portable altar that is made of cloth decorated with scenes from the Passion (Easter Orthodox Christian)

Antiochene School – emphasized humanity of Christ

Aparche (first-fruits) - agricultural gifts to gods (Greek)

Apocalypticism – belief in the sudden ending of world with God's judgment

Apocatastasis – belief that all beings will be reconciled with God in the end (including devil)

Apocrypha – books not included in Hebrew canon or the Protestant canon of the Old Testament but included in Greek Septuagint, Catholic, and Orthodox

Apologetics – Christians focused on defending the reasonableness of Christianity

Apostle – missionaries sent by Jesus (including his disciples and Paul)

Apostolic Fathers – Christian leaders that weren't apostles but either related or close friends with

Apostolic succession – the authority of clergy comes from the unbroken succession between ordinations beginning with the apostles

Arahat – Buddhist monk

Aramaic – a dead Semitic language

Archbishop – Catholic and Anglicanism a bishop that oversees other bishops

Arhat – one who has attained Nirvana (Buddhism)

Arianism – belief by Arius (4th century) that Christ was created by God, greater than a man, less than God

Ark – cabinet in synagogue that holds Torah (Jewish)

Artha – power gain, a permissible goal in life (Hindu)

Arya Samaj – Back to the vedas movement in 1875

Aryans – (Indo-Europeans) semi-nomadic people who migrated from Eastern Europe and greatly influenced India today

Ashera – Canaanite goddess of fertility

Ashkenazim – Jews from the west, central, and east Europe.

Ashramas – the four stages of life (student, householder, hermit, homeless wanderer)

Ashtanga Yoga (Raja Yoga)– Yoga with eight components; morality, ethics, posture, breath control, sense control, concentration, meditation, absorption

Ashtoreth – fertility goddess

Asita – astrologer that predicted Buddha's fate

Asoka – first of the Mauryan emperors of India, sponsored Buddhist teachings in rocks, pillars, and caves

Assimilation - the merging of cultural traits from previously distinct cultural group

Astrology – prediction of lives based on the stars and planets

Asuras – demigods who live in lower heavens, second highest realm (Mahayana Buddhism)

Asvamedha – Aryan horse sacrifice

Atharva-Veda – Brahmanic poetry to meet needs

Atheist – someone who does not believe in any God

Atman- Brahmanic definition of the soul

Avataras – alternate forms assumed by a god

Avidya – ignorance

Avalokita – Indian deity of compassion recognized by Buddhists as bodhisattva

Baal – nature deity common in west Semitic world

Bagua – Taoism eight-trigram schema of proportional combinations of the yang and yin

Baptism – admission into Christian church by immersing, or anointing with water

Baptists – one of the largest Protestant denominations, rooted from the Anabaptist movement. Rejects infant baptism

Bar Kochba – "son of the star" leaders of the second rebellion against Hadrian

Bar mitzvah – Jewish boy coming of age (13) after this age he is expected to obey the commandments

Bat mitzvah – Jewish girl coming of age (12) after this age she is expected to obey the commandments

Bardo – Tibetan term for the period between death and re-birth

Basho – Japanese Zen monk known for Haiku poetry

Bet din – Rabbi court

Bhagavad Gita – "Song of the Blessed Lord", ways of salvation (bhakti – Hindu)

Bhagavad Purana – epic that depicts Krishna as child wonder-worker, lover, king

Bhakti – devotion (the Way of Devotion, the most popular Hindu way to salvation)

Bhikshu – Buddhist monk

Bhikshuni – Buddhist nun

Bishop – priest of a diocese (Catholic)

Bodhidharma – founder of the Zen tradition

Bodhi – Buddhist term for enlightenment

Bodhi tree – fig tree where Buddha sat when he reached enlightenment

Bodhidarmma – monk that brought Buddhism to China

Bodhisattva – an enlightened being (Buddha) that chooses to stay and help others find enlightenment (saint)

Bonpu – in Zen an expression of layperson as opposed to enlightened one

Brahma – the creator (masculine)

Brahman – the world's soul

Brahmanas – portions of the Vedas that discuss the power of Brahmanic ritual to control the gods

Brahman-Atman- indicates the needed identity of the world with the individual consciousness

Brahmo Samaj – religious reform founded by Ram Mohan Roy in 1828 blending Hinduism and Christian ideals

Breviary – book containing liturgy of the Roman Catholic Church

Brihaspati – ritual deity representing the power of prayer

Bris – name for the circumcision ceremony

Brit – covenant between God and Jewish people

Brit milah – see **brit**

Buddha – "awakened" title given to those that achieve perfect illumination (given to Gautama after his enlightenment)

Bushido – samurai code of ethics

Canon – group of writings considered authoritative.

Canonical – belonging to the accepted body of scriptures

Canonize – to declare a dead Christian to be a saint. For Catholics the pope is the only one with this authority, and the Christian must have performed two miracles. For Orthodox they are canonized by regional bishops. Protestants don't canonize.

Canaanites – mostly Semitic population west of Jordan

Catechism – Christian class taken as a precursor to confirmation or baptism

Catholic – term used for the Christian faith until the west and east split. The West retained the Catholic name while the East assumed the name Orthodox

CE – "Common Era" or "Christian Era" to avoid the affirmation of faith in AD (anno domini – meaning "year of our Lord")

Celebrant – Christian priest or minister who presides over service and Eucharist

Chado – tea ceremony in Zen Buddhism to help overcome ordinary consciousness

Chanukah – candlestick with nine branches used in Hanukah ceremony (a.k.a. **menorah**)

Chasuble – garment worn by bishops and priests celebrating Eucharist

Chthonian forces – gods living under the earth

Chukkim – commandments without a known reason (Jewish)

Chun Qiu – Confucian classic – the *Annals of Spring and Autumn*

Chuppah – (aka **huppah**) canopy where a ceremony of marriage takes place

Chutzpah – Jewish compliment of guts or arrogance

Confession – admission of sin either directly to God in prayer, to the congregation, or privately to a priest

Confirmation – one of seven Catholic sacraments (also some Protestant churches recognize) a baptized young adult (about 13) confirms their commitment to the Christian faith

Copts – native Egyptian Christian

Counting of the Omer – Jewish counting of the days between Passover and Shavuot

Crucifier – Acolyte who carries the cross in church procession

Crusades – wars fought against enemies of Christian faith

Cult of the saints – veneration of saints, prayers addressed to them in hopes they'll intercede with God on their behalf (Catholic)

Curate – Assistant pastor who visits the sick -Anglicanism

Daf Yomi – Jewish practice of studying one page of Talmud per day

Daimon – a person's inward moral guardian

Dalai Lama – "ocean measureless superior one" head of the Gelukpa (Yellow) Tibetan Buddhism

Dao – the way (Taoism/Daoism)

Dao De Jin – the text of Daoism

Dasas- indigenous people of northwest India that were invaded and subdued by the Aryans

Da Xue – the *Great Learning* treatise for young gentlemen education (Confucian)

De – Daoism for power

Deity – a being that is worshipped

Deuteronomic Reform – cleansing of ritual and moral life under King Josiah 621 B.C.E.

Devi – Hindu Mother Goddess

Dharma – "foundation" truth and duty, teachings of Buddha

Dhyana – meditation into another consciousness (Buddhism)

Dhyani Buddhas – contemplative celestial Buddhas that minister human needs

Diaspora – Jews that live outside Israel

Diocese – geographical region led by a bishop (Catholic)

Divination – uses religion to predict future

Doctrine - body of religious teachings

Documentary Hypothesis – idea that the Torah (Jewish) written by four authors (J – Jehovah, E- Elohim, P – Priestly, D – Deuternomist) Fifth was an editor Redactor.

Dogma - an authoritative principle, belief, or statement of ideas or opinion, especially one considered to be absolutely true

Dosojin – often sexually explicit pillars of stone intended to ensure fertility and protection

Doxology – short hymn celebrating God (Christian)

Dravidians – dark-skinned family in south India not related to the Aryans

Druid – member of the Celtic order of priests/magicians who worshipped animals and trees (and may have partook in human sacrifice)

Dualism – belief that reality is made of two different principles (spirit and matter)

Dunkha – "sorrow" the constant rebirth-re-death cycle

Durga – (**Kali**) fearsome, benevolent goddess (consort of Shiva)

Dvaita – Hindu duality

Dynamic Monarchianism – see **adoptionism**

Ebionites – ascetic Jewish Christians that believed Jesus was a human prophet and upheld law of Moses

Ecumenical council – Christian meeting with several heads of churches

Ekklesia- assembly of people bound by common purpose (Christian 'people of God')

El – common term for superhuman being

Elohim – name for God in Hebrew scripture

El-Shaddai – name for God, especially in reference to Abraham

Eschatology – branch of Christian theology dealing with the end times

Essenes – an ascetic Jewish sect

Eucharist – Lord's Supper, sacrament recognized by all branches of Christian religions

Exegesis - critical explanation or interpretation of a text in the Bible

Excommunication – penalty from Catholic Church that bans a person from receiving or administering sacraments

Fable – short Greek story that shares a lesson (moral)

Fa-jia – Confucian *School of Laws* (legalism)

Fall – (The Fall) disobedience of Adam and Eve

Feng-shui – five elements divination

Five aggregates – Buddhism five aspects that make up humans appearance; human composition, sensation, perceptions, mental formation, and consciousness (**koan**)

Five deadly sins –Buddhism belief that offense cause rebirth in hell; patricide, matricide, killing an arhat, injuring a Buddha, creating schism in the sangha

Five hindrances – Buddhism the five obstacles that must be removed to achieve enlightenment; desire, anger, sloth, worry, doubt

Fundamentalism - religious movement that returns to fundamental (basic) principles, by rigid adherence and often by intolerance of other views and opposition to secularism

Fu-xi – mythical emperor with a serpent body (Taoism/Daoism)

Ganesh – Hindu God of wisdom and good fortune (head of an elephant, and pot belly)

Gautama – founder of Buddhism, clan name of Prince Siddhartha, given name of the historical Buddha

Gemara – secondary portion of Talmud

Genius – a male spirit or daimon who leads

Get – Jewish divorce decree

Gezeriah – Rabbi law to prevent accidental violation of mitzvah

Gohei – Shinto offertory

Gopis – milkmaids and young wives (Hindu)

Gospel – content of Christian teaching, when capitalized it refers to one of the books in the Bible

Goy – non Jew

Gui – earthly yin spirits

Guan-yin or Kwan-yin – Chinese goddess bodhisattva of mercy (Indian: Avalokita, Japan: Kannon)

Guna – quality or attribute (Hindu)

Guru – spiritual guide

Haggadah – oral tradition (Jewish)

Hagiography – biography of a saint

Halakah – formal portion of Talmudic tradition (Jewish)

Hanif –Arabic term for pre-Islamic non-Jewish or non-Christian Arabian monotheists during Prophet (Muhammad) time

Hanukkah – (aka **Chanukah**) eight day Jewish celebration beginning in mid-December commemorating revolt of Maccabees and the oil that burned for eight days

Harijans – "Children of God" Ghandi's term for the untouchable caste

Hashem – Jewish name for God used to avoid saying the name of God

Hashkiveinu – Jewish prayer for protection while sleeping

Hasidim – "pious ones" Jewish sect

Hatha Yoga – Yoga focusing on bodily postures for meditation

Hechsher – Jewish "Seal of Approval" on kosher foods

Hellenists – New Testament usage (Acts) Christians of Gentile origin, but absorbed Greek culture (liberals as opposed to Judaizers)

Henotheism – during rituals the god being celebrated temporarily rises to most powerful of the gods while the others are ignored to flatter the god

Hermeneutics – science of explanation in theology that deal with Biblical interpretation.

Hieros gamos (holy marriage) – Greek celebration of marriage between Zeus and Hera (aka **Theogamia**)

Hinayana – "lesser vehicle" name applied to early Buddhists (today they are the **Theravadins**)

Homer – author of Greek epic poems Iliad and Odyssey

Hui-neng – last leader of the Zen movement in China

Hun – shen soul, seat of the mind (Taoism)

Imitative magic - magic that attempts to control the universe through the mimicking of a desired event

Immaculate Conception – Virgin Mary bore Jesus without original sin

Incarnation – the concept of a god appearing in human form (e.g. Jesus)

Indra – Early Hindu god of storms

Ise – peninsula on eastern shore of Japan where first shrine to Amaterasu was

Izanagi and Izanami – "he who invites" and "she who invites" primal god founders of Japan and its people

Jataka – "birth story" folk stories of lives lived well by animals, demons, and humans representing Buddha or other Buddhist prominent figures

Jinja – basic term for Shinto shrines

Jati – birth family (sub-caste)

Jiva – vitality, atman, soul

Jnana – knowledge or understanding (Way Knowledge) Hindu

Jodo – Japanese Pure Land school of Buddhism (China-Jing-tu)

Judaizers – Christians of Jewish background who believed that the Law should be required of all converts (conservatives as opposed to Hellenists)

Jun-zi – morally superior man (Confucian)

Juno – a female spirit who works with the genius

Kabbala – speculative theology, occult symbolism, mystical practice prevalent in Europe and Middle East

Kaddish- Jewish mourners prayer

Kali – (**Durga**) Divine Mother and fierce to demons

Kami – Shinto for upper beings, deities, and spirits

Kalpa – aeon or world age in cycle of creation and destruction of the world over and over again

Kama – one of the four Hindu goals (goal of pleasure) love god shoots flower arrows

Karaites – "readers" movement in Judaism (back to the written law)

Karma – deeds that reflect the effect of later lot in life

Karma-marga – Hindu path of works for salvation

Karuna – compassionate love (Buddhist)

Kashrut – Jewish dietary laws

Kippah – Jewish disc head covering

Koan – tempt, frustrate rational thought through a brief story in Zen meditation

Kojiki – oldest Japanese text on Shintoism

Kosher – food fit to eat (Jewish)

Krishna – avatar of Vishnu, mischievous child, lover of gopis (warrior king)

Kshatriyas (Rajanyas) – Warrior class of castes in early India represented second most powerful

Kuan Yin – female bodhisattva of mercy and compassion worth of worship similar to Virgin Mary for Catholicism

Kundalini – Hindu belief of spiritual snake living at base of human spine, through Yoga is awakened for spiritual and mystical powers

Kyoha Shinto – Shinto faith group

Lakshmi – Hindu goddess of good fortune (favorite wife of Vishnu)

Lama – superior one, Buddhist spiritual leader

Lao-zi – author of the Daoist classic *Dao De Jing*

Li Ji – Confucian *Book of Rites*

Lingam – phallic symbol for Shiva

Logos – "word", in Gospel of John Jesus is referred to as the purpose of God to become manifested in Christ

Lotus position – special prayer position

Luther, Martin – (1483-1546) German monk that questioned church and ultimately was key in the Protestant Reformation

Lun Yu – *Analects* (Confucian sayings)

Maccabees –heroes of a successful rebellion from the Hellenistic Seleucid rule (165 B.C.E.) headed an independent Jewish state until the Romans came in 63 B.C.E.

Madhyamika – "middle" between being and not being (difference between samsara and Nirvana)

Magga – Buddhism fourth Noble Truth – following eight-fold path to enlightenment is how to end suffering

Mahabharata – Indian epic about five Pandava brothers

Mahabhuta – Hindu five great elements – earth, water, air, fire, and ether

Mahayana – "great vehicle" Buddhist sect in India

Mana - force or power, which may be concentrated in objects or persons

Mandala – "sacred circle" chart used for meditation in Tantric Buddhism

Mantras – incantations (common in Tantric Buddhism)

Manu – Hindu name of mythic father of human race (*The Code of Manu* made human Hindu law)

Manushi Buddhas – Buddhas who have become human, taught others, and returned to Nirvana

Mara – Hindu evil

Mashgiach- Rabbi trained to certify food as kosher

Matsuri – Japanese for festival

Matzah – (aka matxo, mazzah) unleavened bread used in Passover

Maya – conscious illusion-making power

Mazel tov – Jewish congratulations, or good luck

Menorah – seven branch candlestick, symbol of Israel

Metta – Buddhism kindness and goodwill

Mezuzah – small parchment of Torah verses placed on Jewish homes door posts

Midrash – "commentary" exposition of a passage (Jewish)

Middle Way – Buddhism advocated lifestyle, balance between asceticism and hedonism

Mikoshi – Shinto portable shrines that were used for matsuri (festivals)

Mikva – Jewish body of natural water used to cleanse

Milarepa – Tibetan poet saint

Minyan – quota of ten Jewish adults required for certain prayers and observances

Mishneh Torah – Deuteronomy book (Jewish)

Mitre – bishop headdress

Mitzvoth – Hebrew commandments

Mlecchas – Hindu for foreigners

Mohel – person that performs Jewish circumcision

Moira – Greek for fate

Mondo – Zen training material (dialogue)

Moksha – release from the cycle of samsara (reincarnation)

Monism – reality is made up of one substance, seeing the dualism in all things

Monotheism – the belief in one God

Mudra – symbolic gesture Buddhism (hand gesture or token)

Nabi – Judaism prophet

Nagarjuna – author of part of the Mahhyamika from the "middle doctrine" school Buddhism

Namaste – Hindu greeting with spiritual significance

Nembutsu - Mantra of Japanese Buddhism sect

Neophyte – recently baptized Christian

Nichiren – "Sun Lotus" nationalistic Japanese Buddhist sect

Niorodha – Buddhism end of suffering through nirvana (third of Four Noble Truths)

Nirvana – "cooled" the release from the rebirth-re-death cycle

Niyama – moral what should be done (Hindu)

Nontheism – unconcerned with supernatural

Numen – the divine part of a person

Officiant – minister presiding over service that does not include the Eucharist (Christian)

Olem Ha-Ba – Jewish afterlife

Oracle- a being that gives revelations of what is to come or of what needs to be done

Orthodox – people that follow an established religious tradition through literal interpretation of scripture

Pali – ancient Indic tongue used in the Theravada (Hinayanan) scripture

Panchatantra – Hindu animal fables depicting lessons

Pantheism – everything in the universe is divine

Pantheon – a set of beings (gods) typically within a region

Parinirvana – "final" Nirvana

Paritta – Buddhist healing and blessing rite

Passion – crucifixion of Jesus and the event preceding

Passover – eight-day festival celebrating the escape of the Jews from Egypt

Patanjali – author of *Yogasutras* significant in Yoga philosophy

Peng-lai – Taoism mythical island where magic mushrooms exist that give immortality

Pentecost – (Judaism) harvest festival, Shebhuoth, fifty days after Passover. (Christianity) seventh Sunday after Easter to celebrate Holy Spirit among assembly

Pentateuch – first five books of the bible (written by Moses)

Pharisees –Jewish sect that advocated stringent application of Jewish law, accepted ideas of resurrection and oral tradition

Po – gui soul, afterlife dwelling in the earth (Taoism)

Polytheism – the belief in many gods.

Prajna – wisdom

Prajna-paramita – female personification of wisdom (Tantric Buddhism)

Prakriti – nature

Prasad – an offering (usually food) given to a god, then eaten by the worshipper

Pretas – Mahayana Buddhist belief in hungry ghosts existing in lower realms depicted with small mouths and large stomachs hunger never satiated

Pu – uncarved block, Taoism representation of perfection in its natural state

Pure Land Buddhism – Mahayana Buddhism belief that through grace of Amida believers will be reborn into Pure Land paradise (most popular form in Japan)

Pudgala – Buddhism semi permanent but perishable

Puja – worship

Puranas – Hindu epics, collections of stories about gods and sages

Purusha – original cosmic in Hindu culture

"Q" (Quelle) – hypothetical collection of sayings of Jesus

Qi – Confucian vital energy

Qibla – the direction a Muslim should be facing during prayer

Quinquagesima – Sunday before Ash Wednesday (Christian)

Rabbi – Jewish spiritual leader

Rajas – one of three gunas (red, restless, impetuous)

Rakan – Japanese for arhat

Ramakrishna – Hindu that proclaimed oneness of all religions

Ramanuja – authored theistic Vedanta school

Ramayana – epic of struggles of Rama and his allies when rescuing Sita from the demon Ravana

Ranto – Tower of the tomb of a Zen monk

Ren – Confucian benevolence

Rig-Veda – oldest portion of Brahmanic sacred literature uses as a guide for Aryan priests

Rosary – Catholic practice of Hail Mary with the use of rosary beads

Roshi – Zen spiritual leader

Ru jiao – Confucian way of educating gentlemen

Rosh Hashanah – Jewish new year

Rudra – (later Shiva) mountain-god feared and revered, could destroy or heal

Sacrament – solemn Christian ritual Catholics have seven (baptism, confirmation, Eucharist (communion), penance, extreme untion, ordination, marriage) the Protestants only recognize baptism and the Eucharist as sacraments.

Sadducees – rejected oral tradition in Judaism, heeded only what was written in Jewish law

Sadhu – Hindu holy man that renounces material world wandering place to place with nothing

Saint – for Protestants any Christian believer for Catholics a holy Christian who meets certain requirements

Saivism – Hindu sect that worships Shiva, worshipers typically covered in ashes, with long hair, and three horizontal markers on foreheads

Sandek – Jewish godfather, the one that holds the baby during the circumcision ceremony

Sankhya – dualist view believing the eternal separateness of reality of matter and spirit

Sanhedrin – supreme judicial, religious, and political body of Judaism during Roman rule

Samadhi – trance in yogic practice

Samsara – reincarnation

Samudaya – second of Four Noble Truths – suffering caused by desire

San Jiao – "Three Religions" period that tried to combine: Daoism, Confucianism, and Buddhism

Sangha – "assembly" monk or nun clan

Sannyasin – someone who renounces earthly ties, and is the final stage of the ashramas. The male wanders alone begging for food. His sole concentration is to be released from the samsara.

Sanskrit – an Indo-European, Indic language associated with religious and classical literary language of India

Sati – a virtuous widow who was cremated to join her dead husband

Satori – Zen term for enlightenment

Sattva – gunas white, light, and intelligent

Satyagraha- non-violent resistance for political reform (as practiced by Gandhi)

Seder – meal during Passover (usually on first of second day) celebrating the release of the Jews from Egypt

Sephardim – Jews from Spain, Mediterranean, and Middle Eastern areas

Septuagint – Greek version of Hebrew scriptures

Shang Di – upper ruler of heaven (Taoism)

Shaktism – Hindu sect devoted to worship of divine female power (Sakti)

Shakti – cosmic energy

Shakyamuni – "sage of the Shakyas" title appled to Gautama Siddhartha in history

Shalom- Hebrew hello, goodbye, or peace

Shaman – a person who is the intermediary between natural and supernatural worlds (using magic to cure, foretelling future, controlling spiritual forces)

Shankara – non-dualist interpretation of Vedanta

Shekhinah – Jewish presence of God (Kabbalism belief of feminine aspect of God)

Shen – heavenly yang spirits

Sheol – Jewish world of the dead

Shi – power through rank, position, or natural circumstance

Shi Jing – Confucian *Book of Poetry*

Shiva – major Hindu god, destroyer/creator

Shochet – kosher butcher

Shotoku – Prince who introduced Buddhism to the Japanese

Shruti – what is heard in Brahmanic literature, transmission of the Vedas

Shu – altruism

Shu Jing – Confucian *Book of History*

Shudra – lowest ranking caste in early Hindu culture (the slaves)

Siddhartha – "goal attainer" name of the prince who later assumed the name Buddha Gautama

Skandhas – "heaps" five impermanent collectives (form, feeling, conception, karmic dispositions, consciousness) causing a mistaken sense of self (Buddhist)

Shakti- Hindu Great Goddess consort of Shiva

Sila – Buddhist obligations (monks and nuns adhere to all ten, laypersons to the first five) – Ten Precepts.

Smriti – what is remembered, sacred writings for Hindus that are created by people

Soka Gakkai- more modern Japanese Buddhist movement

Soma – sacred drink in early Hinduism

Stations of the Cross – fourteen events in the Passion of Christ, they are sources of devotion for Catholics

Stupa – Buddhist circular tower that is used for devotion

Sun Zhongshan – founder of the Republic of China (1912) sought blend of socialist and democracy

Sunyata – emptiness (Buddhism term)

Svarodaya – science of breath control in yoga

Synagogue – Jewish church

Synoptic Gospels – New Testament books Matthew, Mark, and Luke that have similar views of Christ's life

Tanakh – Jewish bible

Tantric Buddhism – kind of Buddhism characterized by a male/female polarity

Tapas – Hindu for heat, one of the five niyamas

Tea Ceremony – Buddhist ritual to overcome consciousness

Terayfa – food that is not kosher that Jews cannot eat (**treyf**)

Tai Ji – Confucian the Great Ultimate

Talmud – collection of Rabbinic oral traditions (Jewish)

Tamas – dark guna heavy and dull

Tammuz (Adonis) – Mesopotamian god of vegetation and fertility

Tanha – "thirst" the cause of rebirth due to the desire and craving.

Tantra – "extension" Buddhist and Hindu manuals (including mantras) to help personify the religion

Tapas – psychic heath/energy generated by asceticism

Tara – female Buddhist protective divinity

Tathagata – self-reference used by Buddha that is
	deliberately non-descriptive

Tendai – Buddhist schools that favored Lotus Sutra but
	harmonized on many levels of the Trikaya

Theravada – "way of the elders" one of the Hinayana
	schools of Sri-Lanka, referred today as the tradition
	of Pali Buddhism.

Theogony – the story of the origin of the gods

Three Fires (Three Poisons) – Buddhist causes of
	suffering

Tian – heaven or sky (Taosim)

Tithe – a monetary offering to a god

Torah – Jewish theology as a whole (first five books of
	Jewish bible)

Transubstantiation – belief that bread and wine actually
	becomes body and blood of Christ

Transfiguration – event where Peter, James, and John saw
	Jesus transformed into glowing heavenly figure
	talking with Elijah and Moses

Trikaya – "Triple Body" the Buddha – Absolute body
	(bliss), Bliss/Enjoyment body, and Condescension
	body (transformed to human)

Trimurti – Hindu belief that Brahma, Vishnu, Shiva are
	three forms of Ultimate Reality

Trinity – the Christian doctrine of the unity of the Father,
	Son, and Holy Spirit into one God

Tripitaka – "three baskets" early Buddhist scripture including Vinaya (monastic rules), Sutta (discourses), and Abhidhamma (supplementary philosophical doctrines)

Trishna – Buddhist thirst/craving/desire

Ummah – a term used for entire Muslim community

Unitarianism – Christian belief that rejects the Trinity

Universalism – belief that all souls will go to heaven

Upanishads – "to sit near a teacher" philosophical meanings of the Vedas

Upali – first monk ordained by Buddha

Upaya – Tantric Buddhist "compassion in action"

Ushas – early Hindu goddess of dawn

Vairocana – Buddha of effluent light (sun) center of the Tantric Buddhist

Vaisnava – Hindu follower of god Vishnu

Vaisyas – third caste of early India comprised of the merchants and artisans

Vajrayana – Buddhist term for fast sudden insight

Varuna – Vedic god of night sky and keeper of morals

Veda – Brahmanic early poems and hymns

Vedanta – the conclusion of the Vedas

Vicar of Christ – another name for the Pope

Vijnana – consciousness

Vinaya pitaka - Buddhist code of behavior for monks

Vipaka – consequences

Vipashyana (vipassana) - insight

Virgin Birth – belief that Jesus had no human father

Vishnu – major Hindu god "preserver"

Vishisht-advaita – branch of Vedanta associated with Ramanuja

White Lotus School – Buddhist sect focusing on the Lotus Sutra

Wounds, Five Sacred – five wounds of Christ suffered through the crucifixion (hands, feet, and side)

Wyrd – chance, fate, destiny

Xian – Daoist sage immortals

Xiao – Confucianism filial piety

Xin – one of the Confucian Five Virtues – faith

Yajur Veda – second book of the Veda containing ritual instructions and hymns

Yahweh – name of god in sacred tetragram (Hebrew)

Yama – Buddhist king of the 21 hells, for Hindus this term is equivalent to the western term "sin"

Yang – active, warm, dry, masculine symbol (opposite of yin)

YHWH- Jewish belief that this is God's sacred name

Yi - one of the Confucian Five Virtues –righteousness

Yidam – mental image of a god for use during meditation

Yin – passive, cool, moist, dark, feminine symbol (opposite of yang)

Yoga – techniques to overcome bondage (one of the six acceptable philosophical systems of Hinduism)

Yogacara – "consciousness only" Mahayana Buddhist

Yom Kippur – Day of Atonement, confession of sins, reconciliation, and repentance, most sacred day of Judaism (Jewish)

Yoni – ring, vaginal emblem encircling the phallic lingam in Shiva

Zazen – sitting meditation in Zen

Zealots – Jewish sect dedicated to rebellion and overthrow of Roman rule in Palestine

Zemban – Buddhism board used for long sessions of Zazen used to prop up the chin during sleepiness

Zen- meditative school of Buddhist in China and Japan (Chinese - Ch'an)

Zendo- hall in which Zen is practiced

Zheng-ming – rectification of names (Confucian) conforming to society ideals

Zhi - one of the Confucian Five Virtues - wisdom

Ziggurat – pyramid structure built by Mesopotamians

Zionism – movement for Jewish nationalism and promotion of welfare Israel

Zohar – major text of the Kabala movement

LIST OF APPENDICES:

Appendix	Description
Appendix A	Major Greek and Roman Gods
Appendix B	Major Hindu Gods
Appendix C	Indian Caste System (Hindu)
Appendix D	Buddhism: A Quick Look
Appendix E	Books of the Bible
Appendix F	Christian Seven Deadly Sins
Appendix G	Christian: Major Denominations
Appendix H	Approximate Percentages of the Examination

APPENDIX A: MAJOR GREEK AND ROMAN GODS

Greek Name	Roman Name	Role
Aphrodite	Venus	Beauty
Apollo	Apollo	Prophecy, medicine (later Greek – sun)
Ares	Mars	War
Artemis	Diana	Hunting (later moon)
Asclepius	Aesculapius	Medicine
Athena	Minerva	Arts, war (later wisdom)
Cronus	Saturn	Ruler of Titans, god of sky (Roman – agriculture)
Demeter	Ceres	Grain
Dionysus	Bacchus	Wine/vegetation
Eros	Cupid	Love
Gaea	Terra	Mother Earth
Hephaestus	Vulcan	Fire
Hera	Juno	Marriage/childbirth: Queen married to Zeus/Jupiter
Hermes	Mercury	Messenger, protector of travelers
Hestia	Vesta	Home guardian
Hypnos	Somnus	Sleep
Hades	Pluto	Underworld/dead
Poseidon	Neptune	Sea and earthquakes
Rhea	Ops	Wife of Cronus/Saturn Mother Goddess
Uranus	Uranus	Sky, father of the Titans
Zeus	Jupiter	Ruler of gods, married to Hera/Juno

APPENDIX B: MAJOR HINDU GODS

God's Name	Significance
Brahma	The Creator (first god in the Hindu trinity) (the others are Vishnu and Shiva). Supreme being (the god of the gods)
Bhairav	Fierce incarnation of Shiva (Avatar)
Ganesha	God of beginnings and knowledge. Child of Shiva and goddess Parvati.
Lord Hanuman	Avatar (incarnation) of Shiva. Represents devotion and dedication. Provides courage, hope, knowledge, and devotion.
Lord Rama	Seventh incarnation of Lord Vishnu. Courtesy, virtue, and morals.
Lord Krishna	Eighth Avatar of Lord Vishnu. Love, divine ecstasy.
Shiva	The Destroyer part of the Trimurti.
Surya	Sun god, only visible god.
Vishnu	The Preserver, part of the Trimurti.

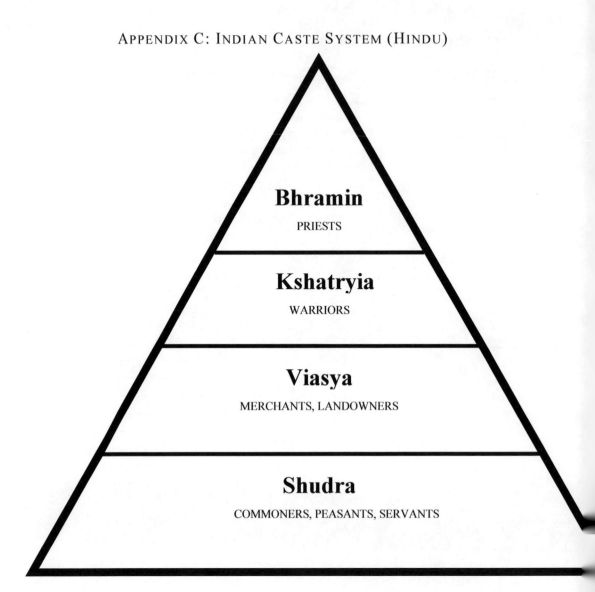

Bhramin
PRIESTS

Kshatryia
WARRIORS

Viasya
MERCHANTS, LANDOWNERS

Shudra
COMMONERS, PEASANTS, SERVANTS

OUTCASTES/UNTOUCHABLES

APPENDIX D: BUDDHISM: A QUICK LOOK

FOUR NOBLE TRUTHS

1. Suffering exists

2. Suffering arises from attachment to desires

3. Suffering ceases when attachment to desires ceases

4. Freedom from suffering is found through the Eightfold Path

NOBLE EIGHTFOLD PATH

Qualities	Eightfold Path
Wisdom (**panna**)	Right View
	Right Thought
Morality (**sila**)	Right Speech
	Right Action
	Right Livelihood
Meditation (**samadhi**)	Right Effort
	Right Mindfulness
	Right Contemplation

THREE CHARACTERISTICS OF EXISTENCE

Characteristic	Translated
Anicca	Transiency
Dukkha	Sorrow
Anatta	Selflessness

BUDDHISM'S VALUES AND VIRTUES

Aspect	Greatest
Achievement	Selflessness
Worth	Self-mastery
Quality	Serving others
Medicine	Emptiness of everything
Action	Nonconformance to worldly ways
Magic	Transmuting passions
Generosity	Non-attachment
Goodness	Peaceful mind
Patience	Humility
Effort	Unconcerned with results
Meditation	Mind that lets go
Wisdom	Seeing through appearances

BUDDHISM'S BELIEFS ON WHAT BINDS US TO SAMSARA (REINCARNATION) AKA. THE TEN FETTERS (SAMYOJANA)

Fetter	Meaning
Drishti	Belief in a separate personality
Vichikitsa	Doubt that has no satisfaction
Silabbata-paramasa	Attachment to rules and rituals without examination
Kama-raga	Sensuous craving
Vyapada	Wishing harm on others
Rupa-rapa	Higher material existence craving
Arupa-raga	Non-material existence craving
Mana	Egotism
Udhacca	Restlessness
Avidya	Ignorance

The Bible was written from about 1450 BC to 100 AD, by many authors and in many places. It consists of the New and Old Testament.

OLD TESTAMENT (ALSO THE JEWISH TANAKH)

In the Old Testament the first five books are scribed by Moses and are said to be the **Pentateuch**.

Book	Message
Genesis	Outlines the beginnings of earth and people, monotheistic, there is no good, all is divine (Moses wrote)
Exodus	Outlines Jew's escape from the Egyptian pharaoh, Moses parting the Red Sea, plagues on Egypt, God's covenant, how to put together the Temple of worship (Moses wrote)
Leviticus	How to worship the Lord and live a Holy Life (offerings, cleanliness, Day of Atonement, and Holy Living rules and regulations) (Moses wrote)
Numbers	Journey to the Promised Land. Three division in book: Israel at Sinai preparing for journey, Israel at Kadesh delayed due ot rebellions, Israel on plains of Moab getting ready to conquest Promised Land. (Moses wrote)
Deuteronomy	Speaks of The Great Commandment (Absolute Allegiance) and leadership succession (last book of the Pentateuch). (Moses wrote)
Joshua	Succeeds Moses as leader of the Israelites as commanded by God.
Judges	Historical account detailing the corruption of Israel and the appointment of judges by God.
Ruth	Historical account of the noble side of Hebrew life.
Samuel 1 and 2	Historical account of David and Saul. The tale of David and Goliath is told in these books.

Book	Message
Chronicles 1 and 2	Historical account of Hebrew history (duplicates much of Samuel and Kings)
Ezra	Historical account of Jewish exiles return after bondage in Babylon.
Nehemiah	Historical account of Jewish exiles return after bondage in Babylon.
Esther	Historical account of the Jews in exile.
Job	Poetical book in the Bible that deals with the problem of human suffering.
Psalms	Poetical book in the Bible of praise.
Proverbs	Poetical book in the Bible filed with short sayings with practical implications.
Ecclesiastes	Poetical book in the Bible
Song of Solomon	Poetical book in the Bible filled with love songs.
Isaiah	Major Prophetical book judgment upon Judah for her sins, and portrayal of Messiah in the Old Testament.
Jeremiah	Major Prophetical book told during the fall of Judah.
Lamentations	Major Prophetical book with five poems lamenting Jerusalem's 586 B.C. capture.
Ezekiel	Major Prophetical book discusses the fall of Judah.
Daniel	Major Prophetical book that talks of the apocolypse.
Hosea	Minor Prophetical book likened God's love to the same kind of love he had for his cheating wife.
Joel	Minor Prophetical book encouraging Judah to repent to save themselves from judgment.
Amos	Minor Prophetical book announcing the impending judgment of God.
Obadiah	Minor Prophetical book mainly denunciating the Edomites.
Jonah	Minor Prophetical book declaring universatility of God's love.
Micah	Minor Prophetical book similar to Amos.
Nahum	Minor Prophetical book predicting the downfall of Nineveh.
Habakkuk	Minor Prophetical book written in the form of prophets' complaints and God's replies.

Book	Message
Zephaniah	Minor Prophetical book discussing judgment and salvation.
Haggai	Minor Prophetical book discussing rebuilding the House of God.
Zechariah	Minor Prophetical book that is apocalyptic.
Malachi	Minor Prophetical book predicts the return of Elijah.

NEW TESTAMENT

Book	Message
Matthew	One of the Four Gospels, most complete account of Jesus' teachings.
Mark	One of the Four Gospels, the shortest of the Gopels, discusses from Jesus' baptism to His ascension. Concentrates on His "mighty works" the most theological of the Gospels.
Luke	One of the Four Gospels presents Jesus as the Universal Savior. This Gospel includes the Virgin Birth.
John	One of the Four Gospels, the most spiritual. Interprets the same events form the other three Gospels with spiritual meaning.
Acts	Historical book recording the history of the Apostolic Church. Tracing through the life and growth of Christianity and the missionaries.
Romans	Apostle Paul's writings to the Christians in Rome. Discuses the universality of sin, impotence of the law for salvation, and natice of God's saving through Christ.
Corinthians 1 and 2	Apostle Paul advises the Corinthian church on spiritual gifts, Christian love, and Resurrection. The second Corinthians discusses the hardships Paul as endured in serving Christ.
Galatians	Apostly Paul's letter to the church in Galatia discussing Christian freedom.
Ephesians	One of Apostle Paul's imprisonment letters (there were four). Discusses the Church's relationship to

Book	Message
	Christ.
Philippians	Apostle Paul's message of joy and the humility of Jesus.
Colossians	Apostly Paul's brief letter on the Lordship of Christ.
Thessalonians 1 and 2	Apostle Paul's letter to the Thessalonian Church concerning the return of Christ.
Timothy 1 and 2	Considered a pastoral epistle addressing the material from the perspective of minister not Church. Timothy discusses qualification of church officers, treatment of widows, and future rewards.
Titus	Personal letter written from Apostle Paul to Titus (young minister he left in Crete). It is a practical letter discussing the current problems that Titus' experiences.
Philemon	Shortest of Paul's letters to Philemon entreating him to accept his runaways slave (Onesimus) back as a brother in Christ.
Hebrews	Attributed to Paul a writing proclaiming Jeus as the great High Priest.
James	Written by James, the most Jewish in style a practical letter dealing with Christian ethics.
Peter 1 and 2	Peter speaking of the persecution of Christians and encourages people to be faithful.
John 1, 2, and 3	I John is written for a group and discussing certainty of eternal life. II John written to an elected lady (could be a church or woman). III John is to Gaius a man commended for hospitality.
Jude	Short letter warning readers against faithlessness.
Revelation	Addressed to seven historical churches the Book of Revelation, this book is seen as a prophecy depicting the events that will cause the end of the age.

APPENDIX F. CHRISTIAN SEVEN DEADLY SINS

- Pride
- Greed
- Lust
- Envy
- Gluttony
- Anger
- Sloth

Denomination	Origins	Significant Differences
Baptists	Smyth, English Separatist in 1609. Roger Williams 1638.	Baptism in adolesence. Usually opposed to alcohol. No authority ca stand between believer and God. Separation of Church and State. Extensive Missionary activity.
Church of Christ (Disciples)	1832	Adult baptism and weekly Lord's supper. Avoids anything not based in the New Testament. Supports scholarly education, and highly tolerant.
Episcopalians	Henry VIII in 1534, Protestant Episcopal Church in U.S. in 1789.	Eucharist, infant baptism, and sacraments are seen as symbolic with actual spirtual effect. References the "Book of Common Prayer".
Jehovah's Witnesses	Founded in 1870 by Charles Taze Name Jehovah's Witnesses adopted in 1931.	Annual lord's meal, baptism by immersion. Meetings held in Kingdom Halls and member's homes with extensive door-to-doo visitations. Strict moral code. Avoids blood transfusions and tobaccos.
Latter-Day Saints (Mormons)	Created by Joseph Smith (1820s) in NY. Smith reported receiving new scripture on golden tablets: The Book of Mormon.	Baptism at age 8, laying of hands, temple rites, baptism for the dead, and marriage for eternity. Strict moral code (tithing, family emphasis). Extensive missionary activity. Chruch restored by God through Joseph Smith.
Lutherans	Martin Luther in Wittenberg, Germany, in 1517, break complete in 1519.	Infant baptism, Lord's Supper, Eucharist. Salvation through faith

Denomination	Origins	Significant Differences
Methodist	John Wesley in 1738, first U.S. deonomination in 1784.	Baptism of infants or adults, and Lord's supper.
Orthodox	In Rome in 1054.	Seven sacraments; infant baptizing, infant anointing, Eucharist, ordination, penance, marriage, anointing the sick. Divorce and remarriage can be permitted. Bishops celibate but priests don't need to be. Emphasizes Christ's resurrection (not the crucifixion). Holy Spirit is from God the Father only.
Pentecostal	Topeka, KS 1901 and Los Angeles 1906.	Speaking in tongues, exorcism, adult baptism, and the Lord's Supper.
Presbyterian	John Knox, 1560	Infant baptism, Lord's Supper, bread and wine symbolize Lord's presence.
Roman Catholics	Jesus	Mass, seven sacraments; baptism, reconciliation, Eucharist, confirmation, marriage, ordination, anointing the sick. Divorce and remarriage not accepted, but annulments are sometimes granted. Celibate clergy. Special veneration for the Virgin Mary.
United Church of Christ	1967	Infant Baptism, Lord's Supper.

Percentage	Curriculum Content
6%	**Definitions and Origins of Religion** • Dimensions • Approaches
6%	**Indigenous Religions** • Native North American traditions • Native South American traditions • Native West African traditions • Native Middle Eastern traditions • Hellenic and Roman traditions • Shintoism
10%	**Hinduism** • Historical development • Doctrine and practice
10%	**Buddhism** • Historical development • Major traditions • Doctrine and practice
6%	**Confucianism** • Historical development • Doctrine and practice
4%	**Taoism** • Historical development • Doctrine and practice

Percentage	Curriculum Content
16%	**Judaism** • Historical development • Denominations • Doctrine and practice
18%	**Christianity** • Historical development • Major Traditions • Doctrine and practice
16%	**Islam** • Historical development • Major Traditions • Doctrine and practice
8%	**Religious Movements** • Before 1000 A.D. • After 1000 A.D.

BONUS TAKING THE RELIGION TEST!

All right, let's take a few minutes and talk about testing. The truth is, that to pass the Introduction to World Religions test, you have to develop two very different sets of skills.

- First, you need to know enough about World Religions (Buddhism, Hinduism, Taoism, Christianity… and all of that stuff) to pass
- But for many of you, just mastering the material will NOT be enough. You will also need to develop your test-taking skills.

There are six things you can do to master your testing skills…

STEP 1. RIGHT NOW - TODAY!

It seems obvious, but the better prepared you are, the more confident you will be…and the more confidence you have, the more you will be able to control your test anxiety. Most of us put off what we fear or dislike…but you need to STUDY…starting NOW, TODAY, not tomorrow.

STEP 2. TOMORROW!

Study is important…study is great…BUT study is NOT enough! Along with study, you must practice. You just can't do too many practice test questions; take the tests in this book (don't cheat on this test, it'll give you a feeling of how much of the information you have a handle on).

Practice accomplishes two things:
- Your skills improve as you master the material, and
- You prove to yourself that you can do this…and it is this self-confidence that will help you control test panic.

STEP 3. THE DAY BEFORE THE TEST!

Spend this day studying the heavily tested stuff, like the Christianity, Islam, and Judaism.

STEP 4. THE NIGHT BEFORE THE TEST!

Plot your time, print your map to the test center, and gather everything you'll need to take the test. Do NOT pull an all-nighter studying (that'll just cost you points), you should know this stuff by now.

STEP 5. THE DAY OF THE TEST

Get up an hour earlier than you think you need.
- Treat yourself to a GOOD breakfast…go out if you like…BUT not fast food. Get the hotcakes and biscuits…no Egg McMuffin this morning.
- Relax, eat, and build up your mental and physical energy.

Yesterday, you calculated how long it would take you to reach the test center. Pick up all your materials and leave 30-40 minutes earlier than you planned. Nothing is more stressful than running late for the test…bad traffic…a wrong turn…bad weather…imagine spending an hour or so engulfed in road rage and then sitting down to take a critical test…not good…not good at all!

STEP 6. FEELING A BIT TENSE?

Here's the scene…you're waiting for the test to begin… you're rested, alert, prepared, and confident (well, sort of). Actually, there's this gnawing sense of insecurity tightening your neck and shoulders. "This is how it always starts", you think…and you feel that first, cool touch of panic.At this point, there are a couple things you can do to ward off those first signs of anxiety.

First, get some more oxygen in your system…
- Close your eyes
- Take a very deep breath and hold it for three or four seconds,
- Now, slowly push it out …push out as much air as you can
- Repeat twice.

Do not do this repeatedly…two or three times is enough. Deep breathing repeatedly causes hyperventilation…that is, you could faint…you want to relax, not pass out!

Next, do a simple "tension release" exercise…
- Close your eyes
- Center your attention of the parts of your body that feel tense.
- Now, tighten up…consciously feel your self becoming more and more rigid…until your muscles in the target area feel like steel bands.
- Now begin to relax, very slowly…will yourself to relax one fiber at a time…and continue to shed the tension until your muscles are totally loose and pliant
- Do it two or three times.

Both these exercises can be done at your desk, even during the test…not a bad idea about halfway through. But to be most effective, you should practice these techniques at home, before the test session.

TAKING THE TEST

Here are four test tips to help you improve your test taking skills and improve your score.

TEST TIP #1 - QUESTION TYPES

Here's the good news...all the questions on the test are multiple choice. All you have to do is pick the right one.

TEST TIP #2 - INTERPRETING PROBLEMS

If you are GREAT at taking tests, then do whatever you always do... of course, if you really are great at taking tests, why are you reading this?

- Step 1: Cover the answers and read the problem once carefully... try to identify what type of problem it is... pick out the OBJECTIVE clause ("According to Greek Mythology most people wind up _____ at death...")

- Step 2: Read the problem AGAIN... this time look for tricks or traps; be alert for negatives ("Who of the following did NOT believe...");

- Step 3: Try to visualize the correct answer without looking at the problem answers.

- Step 4: Check the problem answers and locate your answer. If you don't find a close match, re-read the problem...and re-think your solution, matching each of the test answers against the objective phrase. If you do find a close match, that's good. Just be aware that the people creating the test will often anticipate the most likely wrong answers and present these as possible test solutions...

- Step 5: Select your answer... on a paper and pencil test, mark the answer sheet on a computerized test, select and enter your answer.

- Step 6: Re-read the problem and double check your answer.

TEST TIP #3 – TIME

The first few questions are no problem...you breeze through them and just when you start to feel good, you come to problem five... You read the thing three times... every time you look at it, you come up with a different answer. You strain to remember relevant lectures and reading assignments, you try backing into the answer, you wonder if the question has a typo...and then you realize that 30 minutes have passed and you have hardly started the test...

For most of us, the best approach to handling time is to:
- First, read each question twice...resist the temptation to scan and then answer the question.
- During your first pass, try to identify the problem TYPE and determine exactly what the question is asking.
- On second reading, look for tricks, traps, or unusual conditions.
- Don't get bogged down - if the answer doesn't come within a reasonable time, take a guess and mark the question so you can come back to it later.... and MOVE ON!

TEST TIP #4 - "QUESTIONS AND ANSWERS"

As you take the Test, you will find that each question falls into one of four categories:

- Question Category 1 – I know it! You read the question, you remember the material... you might even recall an example used in the book... and you KNOW that the right answer is "C". Good for you... this is how most of the questions will go…

- Question Category 2 – I know it…maybe! The second type of question is a bit more challenging. After reading the problem, you will be fairly certain that the correct answer is "C". But when you re-read the question, answer "B" will look even better… and heaven help you if you read the question again… now "A" will start looking good! Here's the problem… we all have a tendency to question our own decisions…even our GOOD decisions. BUT be careful… studies show that our FIRST choice is usually the RIGHT choice!

If you KNOW your first answer is wrong, then change it, but

If you're not sure, then go with your first answer! (Don't change one guess with another guess!)

- Question Category 3. This one's really tough... ...just follow these steps...
    o Eliminate any obviously incorrect answers
    o If you've really never heard of an answer, eliminate it (it probably has nothing to do with the material)
    o Look at "nearby" questions for help... The good news is that sometimes, the test questions are grouped together by topic. This means that you may be able to use the information in one question to help you answer another question... just be alert!
    o After you've narrowed down the choices, select the one that you think is the BEST answer... sometimes you may find two or more "right" answers... your job is to decide which is "most right".

- Question Category 4. I don't have a clue...! You read this fourth type of question and you really have no idea what the answer is... in fact, you're not even certain that the question is written in English. Don't despair...just choose an answer... yes, that's right... GUESS! Basically, you lose a little less than 1 point for each wrong answer and for each unanswered question.

The MORAL of this story is...
Don't leave any question blank. If you really don't know the answer, eliminate any obviously incorrect answers and then take your best guess. In fact, even if you are planning to come back to a question later, put down some answer... DO NOT LEAVE ANYTHING BLANK... not even temporarily!

TEST TIP #5 – FINISHING IN STYLE!
OK... you're finished. But just to be sure...
- Check that you have answered all the questions
- Double check your answers for carelessness
- Re-visit questions that you were un-sure about...
- AND END IT!

PRACTICE TEST

If you can answer about half of the questions correctly you should be in good shape. To be safe, strive for a 75% on this examination.

1. What is canon?
    a. Acceptable prayers
    b. The history of a religion
    c. The customs of a religion outlined
    d. Official list of holy scriptures
    e. Rejected scripture material

2. Which of the following is the most sacred day of the year for Judaism?
    a. Hanukah
    b. Yom Kippur
    c. Succoth
    d. Purim
    e. Rosh Hashanah

3. Which of the following describes Muhammad?
    a. Messiah
    b. Prophet
    c. Medicine man
    d. Son of God
    e. Author

4. Who are the Apologetics?
    a. Christians who strive to prove their religion
    b. Sunnis who renounce their religion in the face of persecution (to pray forgiveness later)
    c. A separate sect of Buddhists
    d. A Roman and Greek set of gods just below the Titans
    e. A group of monks that roam the plains pursuing an aesthetic lifstyle

5. Which of the following is not a monotheistic religion?
   a. Christianity
   b. Sunni
   c. Shi'ites
   d. Hellenists
   e. Judaism

6. What is a shaman?
   a. The highest clergy member in Judaism
   b. A medicine man of indigenous religions
   c. A faith healer
   d. Someone who conducts exorcisms
   e. An intermediary between the people and the spirit world

7. All of the following Christian sects do NOT believe in the Trinity except:
   a. Arianism
   b. Mormonism
   c. Jehobah's Wintesses
   d. Baptists
   e. Unitarianism

8. Which of the following is NOT one of the seven deadly sins of Christianity?
   a. Gluttony
   b. Anger
   c. Lust
   d. Greed
   e. Merciless

9. The Protestants disagreed with the Catholics on all of the following except:
   a. Prayer to Saints
   b. Purgatory
   c. Mediator (priest) needed between God and man
   d. Belief in the Trinity
   e. Transubstantiation

10. The belief that everything is divine?
    a. Pantheism
    b. Polytheism
    c. Nontheism
    d. Animism
    e. Monotheism

11. What is an atman?
    a. Medicine man
    b. Synonym for shaman
    c. The soul
    d. Priest that recites Vedas
    e. State of unhappiness in life

12. What is dreamtime?
    a. Trancelike state that Zen practicioners experience
    b. Aborigine word for the time of creation
    c. The polytheism worship of animals
    d. The belief that God communicates through dreams
    e. The idea of once you have dreamt of the divine you are released from the samsara

13. What is the Hindu holiday that lasts five days and is celebrated with a festival of lights?
    a. Mahashivarati
    b. Shiva Ratri
    c. Holi
    d. Diwali
    e. Phagwa

14. Who was the most influential Neo-Confucian teacher?
    a. Mencius (Meng Tzu)
    b. Zhu Xi
    c. Hsun Tzu
    d. Mo Tzu
    e. Lsa Tao

15. In Judaism who is someone who speaks for God?
    a. Rabbi
    b. Monk
    c. Prophet
    d. Messiah
    e. Zealot

16. Which of the following was NOT a Christian Inquisition?
    a. Roman Inquisition
    b. Medieval Inquisition
    c. Portugese Inquisition
    d. Spanish Inquisition
    e. Italian Inquisition

17. Which of the following is NOTone of the Eightfold Path?
    a. Right Livelihood
    b. Right Mindfulness
    c. Right Penance
    d. Right Effort
    e. Right Speech

Use the following for questions 18-22
    I.   Elijah
    II.   Micah
    III. Hosea
    IV.   Amos
    V.   Elisha

18. Encouraged Jehu to start a revolution:
    a. I
    b. II
    c. III
    d. IV
    e. V

19. Prophesized that social sins would be punished:
    a. I
    b. II
    c. III
    d. IV
    e. V

20. Stood against turning Yahweh into a Baal nature religion, Elisha carried on his work as his disciple:
    a. I
    b. II
    c. III
    d. IV
    e. V

21. Literary prophet that had an unfaithful wife (similar to unfaithful followers of the Lord), and forgave:
    a. I
    b. II
    c. III
    d. IV
    e. V

22. Prophesized against prophets that succumb to popularity, and the last prophet for seventy years:
    a. I
    b. II
    c. III
    d. IV
    e. V

23. Which of the following is NOT a stage in the ideal Buddhist life?
    a. Bloodline of a Buddha
    b. Student of religion
    c. Marriage and family life
    d. Focus on religion and other spiritual things
    e. Holy wanderer

24. Which religion believes the cow is a holy creature?
    a. Taoism
    b. Buddhism
    c. Hinduism
    d. Confucianism
    e. Judaism

25. Which of the following was NOT one of the passing sights
    for the Prince in Buddhism?
    a. Diseased man
    b. Infant
    c. Ascetic
    d. Dead man
    e. Old man

Use the following for questions 26-30
    I.   Maktabs
    II.   Mullah
    III.   Mujtahids
    IV.   Kharijites
    V.   Sufis

26. Shi'ite primary school run by the clergy?
    a. I
    b. II
    c. III
    d. IV
    e. V

27. Believed the caliph should be elected upon merit:
    a. I
    b. II
    c. III
    d. IV
    e. V

28. Low-level Shi'ite religious leaders:
    a. I
    b. II
    c. III
    d. IV
    e. V

29. Highest-level religious leader for Shi'ites?
    a. I
    b. II
    c. III
    d. IV
    e. V

30. Islamic mystics:
    a. I
    b. II
    c. III
    d. IV
    e. V

31. Which of the following Jewish holidays is a "Day of Atonement"?
    a. Yom Kippur
    b. Passover
    c. Hannuakah
    d. Rosh Hashonah
    e. Mishnah

32. What is a holy wanderer called?
    a. Ashrama
    b. Brahmacharga
    c. Grastha
    d. Vanaprastha
    e. Sannygasu

33. Which of the following Hindu gods is known as the Destroyer?
    a. Shiva
    b. Vishnu
    c. Krishna
    d. Lakshmi
    e. Brahma

34. Pure Land is a denomination in what religion?
    a. Buddhism
    b. Hinduism
    c. Confucianism
    d. Taoism
    e. Shintoism

35. Who is the leader of the underworld in Greek Mythology?
    a. Pluto
    b. Zeus
    c. Apollo
    d. Hermes
    e. Poseidon

36. Which of the following is NOT one of Buddhism six realms of existence?
    a. Animals
    b. Anti-gods
    c. Humans
    d. Hungry ghosts
    e. Sealife

37. Which of the following are ways that Taoists hope to achieve longevity?

    I.   Feng Shui
    II.   Dietary Practices
    III.   Sexual Restraints
    IV.   Breath Control
    V.   Searching for the Isle of the Blessed

    a. I and IV
    b. I only
    c. III and IV
    d. II, III, and IV
    e. All of the above

38. What is diaspora?
    a. Jews outside of Israel
    b. Converts to Judiaism
    c. Unclean (non-kosher) food
    d. Jewish prayer
    e. A group of rabbis that interpet the Talmud

39. In Greek mythology what is a Siren?
    a. Female warrior
    b. Female monster with snakes for hair
    c. Evil female spirit
    d. Half-man, half-horse creatures that practice astrology
    e. Half-bird, half-woman that sing irresistible songs

40. Which approach to religion studies the relationship between the individual and the religious community?
    a. Neurological Approach to religion
    b. Psychology of Religion
    c. Sociology of Religion
    d. Anthropology of Religion
    e. Literary Approaches to Religion

41. Which of the following is not written about Confucianism?
    a. *Dao De Jing*
    b. *Analects, Lun yu*
    c. *Great Learning, Da Xue*
    d. *Doctrine of the Mean, Zhong Yong*
    e. *Book of Mencius*

Use the following for questions 42-46
I.   Torah
II.   Nebi'im
III.   Tanakh
IV.   Talmud
V.   Mishnah

42. The Jewish Bible:
    a. I
    b. II
    c. III
    d. IV
    e. V

43. The writings of the prophets:
    a. I
    b. II
    c. III
    d. IV
    e. V

44. Literature describing the covenant (fixed canon, and what Christians call the Old Testament):
    a. I
    b. II
    c. III
    d. IV
    e. V

45. A book presenting cases that were ruled on by rabbis:
    a. I
    b. II
    c. III
    d. IV
    e. V

46. This book is made up of the Mishna and Gemara:
    a. I
    b. II
    c. III
    d. IV
    e. V

47. Which of the following is NOT one of the authorized Four Goals in Life according to Hinduism beliefs?
    a. Political aspirations (Pukusha)
    b. Pleasure (Kama)
    c. Status and riches (Artha)
    d. Moral Law (Dharma)
    e. Pursuit of Nirvana (Moksha)

48. Who of the following was NOT one of the Twelve Apostles of Jesus?
    a. John
    b. Andrew
    c. Bartholomew
    d. Gabriel
    e. Simon

49. What is the lowest caste?
    a. Shudra
    b. Untouchable
    c. Kshatriyas
    d. Brahmin
    e. Vaishya

50. What is moksha?
    a. A world age
    b. Sacred drink
    c. Priest of fire
    d. The soul
    e. Release from samsara

51. In Judaism what is the Covenant?
    a. An agreement between God and the Hebrews only
    b. An agreement between the Pharoah and Moses
    c. An agreement between Jews and the Canaanites
    d. An agreement between God and all people
    e. An agreement between the Jewish leaders

52. What is a Jataka?
    a. The three baskets
    b. A move in the art of Samurai
    c. A prayer pose
    d. Story of a Buddhist previous life
    e. Release from the samsara

Use the following for questions 53-57

I.   Brahma
II.   Brahman
III.   Brahmanas
IV.   Brahaman-Atman
V.   Brahmin

53. Commentaries on the Vedas that wield control over gods, nature, and humans?
    a. I
    b. II
    c. III
    d. IV
    e. V

54. Member of the Trimurti (the Creator):
    a. I
    b. II
    c. III
    d. IV
    e. V

55. Term to represent the identity of individual consiousness with the universal World Soul:
    a. I
    b. II
    c. III
    d. IV
    e. V

56. The highest group in the varna ordering society, the priestly class:
    a. I
    b. II
    c. III
    d. IV
    e. V

57. The magical potency of mantras (in later philosophy this term was referred to as the World Soul):
    a. I
    b. II
    c. III
    d. IV
    e. V

58. What is shomerim?
    a. Death ritual
    b. Guards for a dead body
    c. Tearing of clothing when hearing of a loved ones death
    d. Twelve month mourning period
    e. Time between death and burial

59. Which of the following denominations is characterized by a middle way between Catholocism and Protestantism?
    a. Eastern Orthodox
    b. Amish
    c. Episcopalian
    d. Baptists
    e. Mormanism

60. Who is the Greek goddess of love?
    a. Athena
    b. Hera
    c. Maia
    d. Dione
    e. Aphrodite

61. The largest Islamic sect is:
    a. Sunni
    b. Shi'ite
    c. Kharijites
    d. Murjites
    e. Sufi

Use the following for questions 62-66

I.   Buddhism
II.   Hinduism
III.   Judaism
IV.   Christianity
V.   Confucianism

62. Follows the Talmud as law?
    a. I
    b. II
    c. III
    d. IV
    e. V

63. Stresses the importance of propriety and becoming honorable gentlemen?
    a. I
    b. II
    c. III
    d. IV
    e. V

64. Which of the religions did Gautama create?
    a. I
    b. II
    c. III
    d. IV
    e. V

65. Which of the following religions believes that the caste system can be justified through Karma?
   a. I
   b. II
   c. III
   d. IV
   e. V

66. All sects of this religion believe that Jesus was the Messiah:
   a. I
   b. II
   c. III
   d. IV
   e. V

67. Which of the following are not one of the plagues sent by God to the people of Egypt?
   a. Boils
   b. Locusts
   c. Hail
   d. Death of firstborn
   e. Floods

68. What is a Tripitaka?
   a. Name for tantric sleep
   b. Triple body of Buddhist reality
   c. Sacred circle in picture art
   d. The "three baskets" of Buddhism
   e. Symbolic gesture

69. What is a ziggurat?
   a. Pyramid structure
   b. Dieties dwelling under earth
   c. Origin of the gods
   d. Predicting the course of fate
   e. Guiding spirit

70. Bhakti Marga is?
    a. The way of devotion
    b. The way of knowledge
    c. The way of works
    d. A yoga pose
    e. The second step in the eightfold path

71. Which of the following is NOT one of the four divine beings of the Greek universe?
    a. Love
    b. Chaos
    c. Knowledge
    d. Earth
    e. Abyss

72. Buddhism is an offshoot of what religion?
    a. Taoism
    b. Shintoism
    c. Confucianism
    d. Hinduism
    e. Christianity

73. Which Christian denomination is known for its separation from society and rejection of modern technology?
    a. Seventh-day Adventist
    b. Amish
    c. Roman Catholic
    d. Lutheran
    e. Anglican

74. Which is NOT a Four Noble Truth:
    a. Life is suffering
    b. It is important to experience suffering
    c. Suffering comes from attachment
    d. It is possible to end suffering
    e. There is a path (eight-fold) to end suffering

75. Who is the ruler of Heaven according to Taoists?
    a. The Jade Emperor
    b. Zeus
    c. Buddha
    d. An avatar in the shape of a dragon
    e. The Great Ultimate

76. The Samurai is a _____ warrior:
    a. Confucian
    b. Buddhist
    c. Hindu
    d. Taoism
    e. Shinto

77. Popes wear a ceremonial ring called the Ring of:
    a. The Virgin
    b. Saint Peter
    c. The Fisherman
    d. Jesus
    e. The saint of the Pope's choosing

78. Which Christian denomination is known for speaking in tongues?
    a. Quakers
    b. Seventh-day Advenists
    c. Baptists
    d. Lutheran
    e. Pentecostals

79. Which of the following is NOT a Catholic practice?
    a. Confession
    b. Stations of the cross
    c. Last Rites
    d. Speaking in tongues
    e. Veneration of Saints

80. What is a Takkanah?
   a. Law that is put in place to prevent unintentional breaking of mitzvot
   b. Custom that has become a part of religious practice
   c. Second half of the Torah
   d. Commandments
   e. A law that does not come from the Torah

81. What is shraddha?
   a. Death rites
   b. Marriage ceremony
   c. Coming of age for girl
   d. Coming of age for boy
   e. Sacrifice performed at an altar

82. The Hindu god of war and storms:
   a. Rudra
   b. Ushas
   c. Vishnu
   d. Varuna
   e. Indra

83. The Trimuriti is made up of:
   a. Vishnu, Brahma, and Yoni
   b. Shiva, Vishnu, and Krishna
   c. Brahma, Krishna, and Yoni
   d. Krishna, Shiva, and Brahma
   e. Shiva, Brahma, and Vishnu

84. What does Buddha mean?
   a. Follower of the Way
   b. Enlightened One
   c. Wise One
   d. Guru of Knowledge
   e. Teacher

85. The Hebrews believe they are descendents of:
    a. Moses
    b. Abraham
    c. Noah
    d. Matthew
    e. Abel

86. The Trimurti represents?
    a. Creation, Preservation, Destruction
    b. Faith, Hope, Love
    c. Peace, Harmony, Serenity
    d. Birth, Death, Salvation
    e. Animals, Humans, Nature

87. What two books make up the Talmud?
    a. Nebi'im and Torah
    b. Mishnah and Gemara
    c. Mishnah and Nebi'im
    d. Gemarah and Kethubim
    e. Kethubim and Nebi'im

88. Which historic Judaism group were passionate about getting Palestine out from under Roman rule, and believed that rebellion was the answer?
    a. Sadducees
    b. Pharisees
    c. Essenes
    d. Zealots
    e. Herodians

89. In Greek Mythology where do most people wind up after death?
    a. Hades
    b. Tartarus
    c. Elysium
    d. Paradise
    e. Heaven

90. Which of the following is NOT one of the Native American's religious rituals?
    a. Sweat Lodge Ceremony
    b. Vision Quest
    c. Smudging
    d. Séance
    e. Making of Relaions

91. Which of the following is an example of trayf?
    a. Fruits and grains
    b. Ham
    c. Chicken
    d. Salmon
    e. Beef

92. Asoka took Budhhism very seriously, which one of the following did he NOT do?
    a. Persecute non-believers
    b. Fourteen Rock Edicts
    c. Minor Pillar Edicts
    d. Cave Inscriptions
    e. Pillar Inscriptions

93. What is known as righteousness in Confucianism?
    a. Li
    b. Ren/Jen
    c. Hsiao
    d. Yi
    e. Chung

94. Which of the following is NOT a pillar of Islam?
    a. Daily Prayer
    b. Confession of sins
    c. Pilgrimmage to Mecca
    d. Charitable duties
    e. Declaration of faith

95. The Islamic people are called:
    a. Hebrews
    b. Christians
    c. Jews
    d. Muslims
    e. Hindus

96. Which of the following Five Classics is the Classic of Odes?
    a. Shu Ching
    b. Shih Ching
    c. I Ching
    d. Ch'un Ch'iu
    e. Li Ching

97. What food label means that a food is fit for Passover?
    a. K
    b. A circle with a U in the middle
    c. D
    d. P
    e. M

98. Who of the following did NOT pen one of the New Testament's four gospels?
    a. John
    b. Luke
    c. Mark
    d. Matthew
    e. Paul

99. How many folds are in the Buddhist path to enlightenment?
    a. 5
    b. 7
    c. 8
    d. 105
    e. 27

100. A Bodhisattva is:
   a. A female Buddha
   b. A god of fertility for Hindus
   c. Someone who has attained enlightenment but is staying to help others do the same
   d. Atman follower
   e. One of the original Buddha disciples

1. D. The canon is an official list of holy scriptures.

2. B. The most sacred day for Judaism is Yom Kippur.

3. B. Muhammad was a prophet for Islam.

4. A. Apologetics are a group of Christians that try to defend their beliefs with proven facts.

5. D. Hellenists believe in many gods (**polytheism**).

6. E. A shaman is an intermediary between the natural and spirit worlds.

7. D. Baptists believe in the Holy Trinity.

8. E. Mercilessness is not one of the seven deadly sins.

9. D. Both Protestants and Catholics believe in the Trinity.

10. A. Pantheism is the belief in the divinity of everything.

11. C. The atman is the soul.

12. B. Dreamtime is the Aborigine word for creation.

13. D. Diwali is the Hindu New Year celebrated with lights.

14. B. Zhu Xi was the most influential teacher of Neo-Confucianism.

15. C. A prophet speaks for God in Judaism.

16. E. There was no Italian Inquisition.

17. C. Right Penance is not a part of the Eightfold Path.

18. E. Elisha encouraged a violent revolution.

19. D. Amos prophesized that social sins would be punished.

20. A. Elijah stood against the king on turning Yahweh into a nature religion.

21. C. Hosea likened his struggle to the Lord's with his unfaithful wife, but forgiveness prevailed.

22. B. Micah was the last prophet for seventy years.

23. A. The bloodline of a Buddha is not one of the requirements for an ideal life.

24. C. Hindus believe the cow is holy.

25. B. The infant is NOT one of the four passing sights.

26. A. Maktabs are primary Shi'ite schools run by the clergy.

27. D. Kharijites believed the caliphs should be elected upon merit.

28. B. Mullahs are low-level religious leaders.

29. C. Mujtahids are the highest-level religious leaders.

30. E. Islamic mystics are Sufis.

31. A. Yom Kippur is the Jewish holiday that is the Day of Atonement.

32. E. Sannygasu is a holy wanderer.

33. A. Shiva is known as the Destroyer.

34. A. Pure Land is a denomination of Buddhism.

35. A. Pluto is the leader of the underworld (Hades).

36. E. Sealife is not one of the Buddhist realms of existence.

37. E. Fengshui, breath control, sexual and dietary restraint, and the search for the Isle of the Blessed are all ways that Taoists try to increase longevity.

38. A. Jews outside of Israel are called diaspora.

39. E. A siren is half-bird, half-woman that sing irresistible songs.

40. C. The sociology approach to religion studies the relationship between self and the religious community.

41. A. *Dao De Jing* is a book written on Taoism not Confucianism.

42. C. The Tanakh is the Jewish Bible.

43. B. The Nebi'im is the writing of the prophets.

44. A. The Torah is the literature describing the covenant.

45. E. The Mishnah are outlined cases with rulings by rabbis.

46. D. This book is made up of the Mishna and Gemara.

47. A. Political aspirations is not one Hinduisms four goals to life.

48. D. Gabriel was not one of the Twelve Apostles of Jesus.

49. B. The Untouchables are the lowest of the caste system.

50. E. Moksha is the release from the samsara.

51. A. The covenant refers to an agreement between God and Jews (anciently Hebrews) only.

52. D. Jataka is the story of a Buddha's previous life.

53. C. Brahmanas are the rituals that are said to wield control over the gods and nature.

54. A. Brahma is the Creator god, member of the Trimurti.

55. D. Brahman-Atman is a term that indicates the essential identitiy with the individual and the World Soul.

56. E. The Brahmin is a member of the priestly class of society (the highest class in the varna).

57. B. Brahman is the magical potency of mantras (in later philosophy this term was referred to as the World Soul).

58. B. Shomerim are the guards for a dead body.

59. C. Episcapalian is a middle way between Catholocism and Protestantism.

60. E. Aphrodite is the goddess of love.

61. A. The Sunni are the largest Islamic sect.

62. C. The Talmud outlines the laws that Jews abide by.

63. E. Confucianism stresses the creation of gentlemen and propriety.

64. A. Gautama created Buddhism, he was considered the first Buddha.

65. B. Hinduism justifies the caste system by the laws of Karma.

66. D. While Christianity denominations are diverse they are all defined as believing that Jesus was the Messiah.

67. E. Floods were not one of the plagues of Egypt.

68. D. The Triptaka is the "three baskets" of Buddhism (Vinaya, Sutta, Abhidhamma).

69. A. A ziggurat is a pyramid structure erected by the Mesopotamians.

70. A. Bhakti Marga is the way of devotion.

71. C. Knowledge is not one of the divine beings of Greek Mythology.

72. D. Buddhism is an offshoot of Hinduism.

73. B. The Amish are known for the separation from society and rejection of technology.

74. B. The Four Noble Truths do NOT include the importance of feeling suffering.

75. A. The Jade Emperor rules Heaven according to the Taoists.

76. E. The Samurai is a Shinto warrior.

77. C. The Ring of the Fisherman is the ceremonial ring worn by the pope.

78. E. Pentecostals are known for the use of speaking in tongues.

79. D. Catholics do not practice speaking in tongues.

80. E. Takkanah is a law that is not from the Torah.

81. A. Shraddha are death rites.

82. E. Indra is the Hindu god of war and storms.

83. E. The Trimuriti is made up of the Hindu gods Shiva, Brahma, and Vishnu.

84. B. Buddha means Enlightened One.

85. B. Hebrews believe they are descendants of Abraham.

86. A. The Trimurti represents Creation, Preservation, and Destruction.

87. B. The Mishnah and Gemara make up the Talmud.

88. D. Zealots were a historic Judaism group that were passionate about getting Palestine out from under Roman rule, and believed that rebellion was the answer.

89. A. According to Greek Mythology most people wind up in Hades after death.

90. D. A séance is not one of the Native Americans religious rituals.

91. B. Ham is trayf (non-Kosher).

92. A. Asoka did not persecute non-believers.

93. D. Yi is righteousness.

94. B. The confession of sins is not one of the Five Pillars of Islam.

95. D. Islamic people are called Muslims.

96. B. Shih Ching is the Classic of Odes.

97. D. A P on food packaging indicates a food is fit for Passover.

98. E. Paul did not pen one of the four Gospels.

99. C. There are eight folds in the aptly name Eight-Fold Path to enlightenment.

100.C.A bodhisattva is someone who has attained enlightenment, but chooses to stay for awhile to help others.

ABORIGINES, 24
ABRAHAM, 65, 98, 100, 101, 118, 178, 187
ADHVARYU, 30
ADVENT, 93
AGNIDH, 30
AH MUN, 12
AH PUCH, 12
ALLAH, 96, 99, 101, 102
AMATERASU, 27, 109, 122
AMAZONS, 21
AMOS, 69, 146, 163, 183
AN, 17. *SEE* AN
ANABAPTISTS, 90
ANALECTS, 57, 124, 168
ANDREW, 82, 83, 170
ANGLICANISM, 90, 111, 116
ANU, 16, 17
APHRODITE, 20, 23, 108, 140, 172, 185
APOLLO, 20, 140, 167
APSU, 17
ARAHAT, 48
ARES, 20, 22, 140
ARTEMIS, 20, 140
ARTHA, 34, 111, 170
ARURU. *SEE* NINHURSAG
ARYA SAMAJ, 44, 111
ASH WEDNESDAY, 93
ASHRAMAS, 36, 131
ASHURA, 98
ASOKA, 50, 112, 179, 188
ASTROLOGY, 16, 42, 112
ATHARVA-VEDA, 29, 30, 112
ATHENA, 19, 20, 23, 140, 172

ATMAN, 31, 32, 122, 162, 182
AUSTRALIAN ABORIGINALS, 11
AVIDYA, 36, 112, 144
AYATOLLAH, 105
BABYLONIAN MYTHS AND EPICS, 16
BACABS, 11, 14
BARTHOLOMEW, 83, 170
BHAGABAD GITA, 37
BHAKTI MARGA, 37, 175, 186
BODHISATTVAS, 55
BOOK OF MENCIUS, 57, 168
BRAHMA, 40, 41, 114, 135, 141, 166, 171, 177, 185, 187
BRAHMACHARGA, 36
BRAHMAN, 31, 32, 114, 171, 185
BRAHMIN, 30, 43, 44, 48, 170, 171, 185
BRAHMINS, 31, 33, 34, 42
BRAHMO SAMAJ, 43, 114
BUDDHISM, 8, 27, 43, 47, 49, 50, 51, 52, 53, 55, 59, 109, 111, 112, 113, 115, 116, 117, 119, 120, 122, 125, 126, 127, 128, 129, 131, 133, 134, 135, 138, 139, 143, 144, 152, 154, 164, 165, 167, 173, 174, 175, 184, 186
Four Bodhisattva vows, 51

FOUR NOBLE TRUTHS, 52, 53, 127, 131, 143, 186

FOUR PASSING SIGHTS, 47

Four Reminders, 51

PURE LAND, 50, 55, 56, 109, 122, 129, 167, 184

Six Realms of Existence, 52

SIX-YEAR QUEST, 48

Ten Precepts, 48, 133

Three delusions, 51

Three marks of existence, 51

Three Refuges, 52

Three trainings, 51

BUSHIDO CODE, 27

CALIPH, 96, 97, 105, 165

CARNIVAL. *SEE* MARDI GRAS

CATHOLIC, 87, 88, 89, 91, 92, 94, 110, 111, 113, 115, 116, 119, 130, 176

CENTAURS, 21

CERBERUS, 22

CH'UN CH'IU, 57, 180

CHAC, 12

CHEVRA KADDISHA, 80

CHRISTIAN INQUISITIONS, 85

CHRISTIANITY, 8, 43, 82, 85, 86, 87, 91, 92, 110, 128, 153, 154, 161, 173, 175, 186

CHRISTMAS, 92, 93, 94

CHU HSI. *SEE* ZHU XI

CHUNG, 58, 179

CIRCUMCISION, 79

CODE OF MANU, 34, 35, 125

CONFUCIANISM, 8, 50, 57, 58, 59, 60, 131, 137, 152, 164, 167, 168, 173, 175, 179, 182, 184, 186

COUNCIL OF NICEA, 85

CRONUS, 21, 140

CRUCIFIXION, 70, 84, 93, 128, 137

DA XUE. SEE GREAT LEARNING. SEE GREAT LEARNING. SEE GREAT LEARNING

DAO DE JING, 61, 62, 124, 168, 184

DAOISM. *SEE* TAOISM

DEEPAVALI. *SEE* DIWALI

DEMETER, 19, 140

DHARMA, 33, 34, 51, 52, 55, 117, 170

DHARMA SHASTRAS, 33

DIDYMUS. SEE THOMAS

DIONE, 20, 172

DIWALI, 45, 162, 182

DOCTRINE OF THE MEAN, 57, 168

DOSOJIN, 27, 117

DREAMTIME, 24, 182

EA, 17. *SEE* ENKI

EASTER, 93

EID AL-ADHA, 98

EID AL-FITR, 98

EIGHT IMMORTALS, 63

EIGHTFOLD PATH, 53, 143, 163, 182

ELIJAH, 68, 75, 135, 163, 183

ELISHA, 69, 163, 164, 183

ELOAH, 65

ELOHIM. SEE ELOAH.
SEE ELOAH

EL-SHADDAI, 65, 118

ELYSIAN FIELDS,. *SEE*
ELYSIUM

ELYSIAN PLAIN. *SEE*
ELYSIUM

ELYSIUM, 22, 178

ENKI, 16, 17

ENKIDU, 18

ENLIL, 16, 17

EPIPHANY, 92

ESSENES, 71, 118, 178

FAT TUESDAY. SEE
MARDI GRAS

FEAST OF LOTS. *SEE*
PURIM

FENG SHUI, 63, 167

FIVE CLASSICS, 57, 180

FIVE PILLARS OF ISLAM,
99

FLOWER SUNDAY. *SEE*
PALM SUNDAY

GEMARA, 74, 120, 169,
178, 184, 187

GHOST DANCE, 25

GILGAL, 65

GILGAMESH, 18

GOOD FRIDAY, 93

GOSPELS, 91, 134, 188

GRASTHA, 36

GREAT LEARNING, 57,
117, 168

GROS BON ANGE, 26

GURUS, 33, 42

HADES, 20, 22, 140,
178, 184

HADITH, 107

HAJJ, 100

HANBALITE, 107

HANIFITE, 107

HANUKKAH, 75, 121

HARAKIRI, 28

HELLENIC AND ROMAN
TRADITIONS, 11, 152

HERA, 20, 121, 140, 172

HERMES, 19, 20, 23,
140, 167

HERODIANS, 71, 178

HESIOD, 19

HESOID'S THEOGONY
FOUR DIVINE BEINGS,
21

HESTIA, 19, 140

HINDUISM, 8, 29, 30, 32,
33, 37, 40, 42, 43, 45,
114, 133, 138, 152,
154, 164, 167, 170,
173, 175, 186

Four Goals, 34

Ten Commitments, 33

Three Debts, 33

HOLAKA. SEE HOLI

HOLI, 45, 162

HOLOCAUST, 74

HOMER, 19, 121

HOSEA, 69, 73, 146,
163, 183

HOSEINIYEH, 105

HOTAR, 30

HSIAO, 58

HSUN TZU, 60, 162

I CHING, 57, 180

IJMA, 107

IKHLAS, 106

ILIAD, 19, 108, 121

IMAM, 99

IMAMS, 103, 104

INDIGENOUS RELIGIONS,
8, 11, 152

INDRA, 30, 122, 177, 187
ISAIAH, 69, 73, 146
ISHTAR, 16, 18
ISLAM, 8, 43, 86, 96, 98, 99, 100, 102, 103, 106, 153, 154, 179, 182, 188
ITZAMNÁ, 12
IXCHEL, 12
IXTAB, 12
IZANAGI, 27, 122
IZANAMI, 27, 122
JADE EMPEROR, 63, 176, 187
JAMES, 10, 82, 83, 135, 148
JANNA, 103
JANUS, 22, 23
JATI, 45, 122
JEHOVAH, 66, 95, 117, 150
JEN. *SEE* REN
JERUSALEM, 69, 70, 85, 89, 93
JESUS, 82, 83, 84, 85, 91, 92, 93, 94, 95, 101, 108, 110, 118, 122, 124, 128, 129, 135, 137, 170, 174, 176, 184, 186
JIGAI, 28
JIZYA, 97
JNANA MARGA, 36
JOHN, 26, 82, 83, 84, 90, 91, 124, 135, 147, 148, 170, 180
JUDAISM, 8, 65, 72, 73, 74, 79, 86, 123, 127, 128, 130, 131, 138, 153, 154, 160, 161,

163, 164, 170, 173, 178, 182, 187
Conservative, 72, 109
Hasidic, 73
Reform, 45, 72, 117
JUDAS ISCARIOT, 83
JUNO, 23, 122, 140
JUPITER, 19, 22, 23, 70, 140
KALPAS, 32
KAMA, 34, 123, 144, 170
KARMA, 32
KARMA MARGA, 35
KERES, 21
KETHUBIM, 73, 178
KHARAH, 97
KHARIJITES, 105, 165, 173, 183
KI, 17
KIGSU, 17
KOCHBA
Bar, 70, 113
KOCHBA, BAR, 70
KOJIKI, 27, 123
KOSHER, 72, 78, 123, 188
KRISHNA, 41, 113, 123, 141, 166, 177
KSHATRIYAS, 31, 123, 170
KUFFAR, 102
LAHORE, 103
LAST SUPPER, 84
LENT, 92, 93
LI, 58
LI CHING, 57, 180
LUN YU. SEE ANALECTS.
  SEE ANALECTS
MADRASEH, 105
MAHASANGHA, 49

MAHASHIVARATI, 45,
  162
MAHAYANA BUDDHISM,
  55, 112, 125, 129, 138
MAIA, 20, 172
MAKING OF RELATIONS,
  25
MAKTABS, 105, 165, 183
MALIKITE, 107
MANUSHI BUDDHAS, 55,
  125
MARDI GRAS, 93
MARDUK, 16, 17
MARS, 22, 140
MATAR, 29
MATTHEW, 83, 91, 134,
  147, 178, 180
MATTHIAS, 83
MAYANS, 11, 13, 14
MAZZEBAH, 65
MEDUSA, 21
MENCIUS, 59, 60, 162
MENG TZU. *SEE*
  MENCIUS
MERCURY, 23, 140
MESOPOTAMIA, 15, 16,
  17
MICAH, 69, 73, 146,
  163, 183
MINERVA, 23, 140
MISHNAH, 74, 166, 169,
  178, 184, 187
MITZVOT, 74, 78
MO TZU, 60, 162
MOHEL, 79
MOIRA, 21, 126
MOKSHA, 35, 126, 170,
  185
MOSES, 66, 67, 101,
  118, 128, 135, 145,
  170, 178

MOSQUE, 104
MOUNT OLYMPUS, 20
MUHAMMAD, 96, 99,
  101, 102, 103, 106,
  107, 120, 160, 182
MUJTAHIDS, 105
MULLAH, 105
NAMMU, 17
NAMTAR, 18
NANNA, 16, 17
NATIVE MIDDLE
  EASTERN TRADITIONS,
  11, 152
NATIVE NORTH
  AMERICAN
  TRADITIONS, 11, 152
NATIVE SOUTH
  AMERICAN
  TRADITIONS, 11, 152
NEBI'IM, 73, 169, 178,
  184
NEPTUNE, 23, 140
NICHIREN SCHOOL, 50
NINHURSAG, 16, 114
NINMAH, 17. *SEE*
  NINHURSAG
NINTU. *SEE* NINHURSAG
NUMA, 22
OBATALA, 26
ODYSSEY, 19, 121
OLORUN, 26
ORACLES, 23, 65
ORTHODOX, 23, 46, 72,
  79, 87, 89, 93, 110,
  115, 127, 172
OUTCASTES, 46
PALM SUNDAY, 93
PARINARVANA, 49
PASSION SUNDAY. *SEE*
  PALM SUNDA

PASSOVER, 67, 74, 79, 116, 125, 128, 132, 166, 180, 188
PESACH. SEE PASSOVER
PETER. SEE SIMON. SEE SIMON. SEE SIMON. SEE SIMON. SEE SIMON. SEE SIMON. SEE SIMON. SEE SIMON. SEE SIMON. SEE SIMON. SEE SIMON. SEE SIMON. SEE SIMON
PETRO, 26
PHAGWA. SEE HOLI. SEE HOLI
PHARISEES, 71, 128, 178
PILATE, 84
PINDA, 35
PITAR, 29
PLUTO. *SEE* HADES
POSEIDON, 20, 23, 140, 167
PRAJNA, 51
PRAKRITI, 31, 39
PRESBYTERIANISM, 90
PROTESTANT, 87, 89, 94, 110, 112, 116, 124
PUJAS, 33
PURE LAND, 56, 165, 183
PURIM, 75, 160
PURUSHA, 39
QIYAS, 107
QUADIANI, 103
QUIRINUS, 22
QUR'AN, 97, 99, 101, 102, 103
RADA, 26
RAINBOW SERPENT, 24
RAJAH, 29

RAJANYAS. *SEE* KSHATRIYAS
RAJAS, 39, 129
RAMA, 41, 130, 141
RAMADAN, 98, 100
RAMAKRISHNA MOVEMENT, 44
RED HAT, 50
REINCARNATION, 32
RELIGION
  Approaches to, 9
  Basic Dimensions of, 9
REN, 58
REVELATION, 91, 92, 148
RIG-VEDA, 29, 30, 130
ROMAN CATHOLIC, 74, 87, 90, 114, 175
ROSH HASHANAH, 75, 76, 130, 160
RUDRA. *SEE* **SHIVA**
SABBATH, 67, 70, 71, 72, 75, 76, 79, 84
SACRED PIPE, 25
SADDUCEES, 71, 130, 178
SADHU, 42, 43, 130
SALAT, 99
SAMA-VEDA, 29, 30
SAMHITAS, 29
SAMSARA, 32, 131, 144
SAMURAI, 27
SANGHA, 48, 52, 131
SANHEDRIN, 84, 131
SANKHYA SYSTEM, 39
SANNYASINI, 37
SANNYASINS, 42
SANNYGASU, 36, 166, 183
SATTVA, 39, 131
SATYA YUGA, 33

SATYRS, 21
SEPPUKU. SEE HARAKIRI
SEVENERS, 104
SHAFI'ITE, 107
SHAHADA, 99
SHAMAN, 25, 132
SHAMASH. *SEE* UTU
SHARI'AH, 106, 107
SHAYKH, 65
SHIA, 98, 103, 104, 105
SHIH CHING, 57, 180,
  188
SHINTOISM, 11, 27, 109,
  123, 152, 167, 175
SHIVA, 30, 40, 41, 42,
  45, 118, 124, 130,
  131, 132, 133, 135,
  138, 141, 162, 166,
  177, 183, 187
SHOAH. *SEE* HOLOCAUST
SHRADDHA, 35, 187
SHROVE TUESDAY. *SEE*
  MARDI GRAS
SHU CHING, 57, 180
SHUDRA, 46, 133, 170
SHUDRAS, 31
SIDDUR, 78
SIMON, 82, 83, 170
SIRENS, 21
SIX ARTICLES OF FAITH,
  101
SKANDHAS
  jamjna, 52
  rupa, 52
  samskaras, 52
  vedana, 52
  vijnana, 52
SKANDHAS, 52
SMUDGING, 25, 179
STHAVIRAVADA, 49
SUCCOTH, 75

SUFIS, 106, 165, 183
SUMERO-AKKADIAN
  PANTHEON, 16
SUN DANCE CEREMONY,
  25
SUNNI, 98, 106, 161,
  173, 185
SURAS, 99
SUTRAS, 49
SWEAT LODGE
  CEREMONY, 25
TABOO, 9
TALMUD, 74, 75, 109,
  116, 120, 134, 168,
  169, 173, 178, 185
TAMAS, 39, 134
TANTRA, 55, 134
TAOISM, 8, 50, 59, 60,
  61, 63, 112, 116, 119,
  121, 128, 129, 132,
  152, 154, 164, 167,
  175, 176, 184
TAPAS, 33
TARIQAH, 106
TARTARUS, 22, 178
THADDAEUS, 83
THEOSOPHY, 44
THOMAS, 83
TI BON ANGE, 26
TIAMAT. *SEE* ZU
TIAN-TAI, 56
TORAH, 70, 71, 72, 73,
  74, 75, 78, 109, 111,
  117, 126, 135, 169,
  177, 178, 184, 187
TRAYF, 78, 179, 188
TRIMURTI, 40, 135, 141,
  171, 178, 185, 187
TRINITY, 87, 95, 135,
  136, 161, 182
TRIPTAKA, 50, 186

TWELVERS, 103, 104
UJI-GAMI, 27
ULAMA, 105, 107
UNTOUCHABLES. SEE
  OUTCASTES
UPANISHAD, 31, 32
UPAYA, 51
URANUS, 21, 140
USHAS, 30, 136, 177
UTNAPISHTIM, 18
UTU, 16, 17
VAISYAS, 31, 136
VANAPRASTHA, 36, 166
VARNA, 45, 172, 185
VARNA, 31
VARUNA, 30, 136, 177
VEDANTA SYSTEM, 40
VESTA, 19, 22, 23, 140
VISHNU, 30, 40, 41, 123,
  124, 135, 136, 137,
  141, 166, 177, 187
VISION QUEST, 179
VISION QUESTS, 25
VOODOO, 11, 26
WAILING WALL, 71
WILLOW SUNDAY. SEE
  PALM SUNDAY
XIN, 58, 137
XUN ZI. SEE HSUN TZU
YAHWEH, 66, 68, 69,
  137, 164, 183
YAJUR-VEDA, 29, 30

YI, 58
YIN YANG, 61
YOGA SYSTEM, 39
YOGACHARA, 55
YOGINS, 43
YOM KIPPUR, 75, 76,
  77, 138, 160, 166,
  182, 183
YOMI
  Land of, 27
YUGA, 37, 38
  Dvapara, 38
  Kali, 38, 44, 118, 123
  Satya, 37
  Treta, 38
ZAIDITES, 104
ZAKAT, 99
ZEALOTS, 71, 138, 178,
  187
ZEDEKIAH, 69
ZEN, 50, 56, 113, 114,
  115, 121, 123, 126,
  130, 131, 138, 162
ZEUS, 19, 20, 121, 140,
  167, 176
ZHONG YONG. SEE
  DOCTRINE OF THE
  MEAN
ZHU XI, 59, 162, 182
ZIGGURATS, 15
ZU, 17

6725092R0

Made in the USA
Lexington, KY
14 September 2010